# GEORGE III AND LORD BUTE

*This publication, in part,
is sponsored by the*
*University of Connecticut*

*James Lee McKelvey*

---

# GEORGE III AND LORD BUTE

---

THE LEICESTER
HOUSE YEARS

---

Duke University Press
Durham, North Carolina
1973

© 1973, Duke University Press
L.C.C. card no. 72–96682
I.S.B.N. 0–8223–0238–7

PRINTED IN THE UNITED STATES OF
AMERICA BY HERITAGE PRINTERS

# PREFACE

I would like to express my gratitude to the Marquess of Bute for his permission to use the Bute family papers and to Miss Catherine Armet, his archivist, for her scholarly guidance and gracious hospitality.

This study is an outgrowth of my doctoral dissertation at Northwestern University. It owes much to the perceptive criticism and encouragement of my advisor, Lacey Baldwin Smith, and to the continual assistance of George T. Romani. Many others have contributed. Miss Doris Coates of the National Register of Archives in London gave generously of her vast knowledge of British manuscript collections. William W. Abbot permitted me to read his unpublished essay, "Lord Bute takes the Stole." The advice of my colleagues, A. William Hoglund, Robert W. Lougee, Harry J. Marks and R. Kent Newmyer, has solved many textual problems. Carl W. Schaefer, Chairman of the University of Connecticut Publication Series, has used both guile and persistence on behalf of this book. For help on typing and proofreading I would like to thank Miss Frances Stearns, Mrs. R. Kent Newmyer, Mrs. Sharon Mullins, Mrs. S. E. Wollman and the University of Connecticut Research Foundation.

I owe a great debt to librarians. The staffs of the British Museum, the Public Record Office, the Central Library of Cardiff, Deering Library of Northwestern University, the Newberry Library, the University of Edinburgh Library, the Heidelberg College Library, and the Institute of Historical Research, London, have all gone out of their way to ease my task. The Reference Room Staff of the Wilbur Cross Library of the University of Connecticut has been especially helpful in obtaining interlibrary loans for me. I remember particularly the kindness I received at the National Library of Scotland.

Grants from the American Philosophical Society and the University of Connecticut Research Foundation have facilitated the writing and publishing of this book.

My obligation to other historians is obvious, but I should like to acknowledge my reliance on the works of Sir Lewis Namier and Romney Sedgwick. While I do not always agree with their conclusions, their influence necessarily pervades any discussion of Leicester House or the early years of George III.

Without the patience and understanding of my wife, Karen, this book could never have been written.

## CONTENTS

Note on Manuscript Sources  *viii*

Introduction  *ix*

1. Lord Bute and Prince Frederick  3
2. The Emergence of a New Leicester House Faction  14
3. Lord Bute Becomes Groom of the Stole  33
4. The Formation of the Pitt-Newcastle Ministry  48
5. Leicester House and the New Administration  62
6. The Prince and His Favorite  82
7. New Frustrations  103
8. A New Direction at Leicester House?  121

Epilogue  141

Index  143

# NOTE ON MANUSCRIPT SOURCES

The papers of the third Earl of Bute are now divided into three major parts. The largest collection is still in the possession of his descendants and is normally kept at Mountstuart on the Isle of Bute. Many letters to the earl, including over four hundred from George III, are in the Central Library, Cardiff. The British Museum possesses Bute's Letter Book and the Minute of his Correspondence (B.M. Add. MSS 36,796–7), and the Musgrave autograph collection (B.M. Add. MS. 5726) includes many mutilated letters to Bute.

The most important of the other collections pertinent to Leicester House in the 1750's are the Newcastle, Hardwicke and Holdernesse papers in the British Museum, the Chatham Papers in the Public Records Office (30/8/24), and the Minto manuscripts in the National Library of Scotland.

# INTRODUCTION

Recent years have seen numerous writings on the early period of George III's reign. Many represented reactions against the ideas of Sir Lewis Namier, others were counter-blasts by Namier's supporters. This exchange served a useful purpose; the more extreme positions on both sides have now been abandoned by all but the most blatantly partisan. No one, for example, now talks seriously of George III's "tyrannical designs." And on the other hand, most historians are now willing to concede that, while George III may have stayed within the bounds of law, he did violate the "customs" or "usages" of the constitution as they had developed under his three predecessors.

Still unanswered, however, is the problem of George III's intentions at the time of his accession. The difficulty here is the relationship between ideas and practice. Even Namier and his followers acknowledge that George III came to the throne "a man with a mission," obsessed with his "visionary program." But they deny any importance to these facts because, as Namier says, George III's ideas were naive commonplaces, "innocent flapdoodle." Herbert Butterfield, W. R. Fryer and others have replied that ideas can not be dismissed simply for lack of originality, and that George III did, in fact, act on the basis of his ideas.

It is a major contention of the present study that George III ascended the throne on October 25, 1760, as a dedicated man, determined to free the crown from its "bondage" and to bring the blessings of liberty and virtue to his oppressed subjects. Only five years earlier this zealous prince had been an indolent and backward youth, totally uninterested in politics. His transformation resulted from the influence of Lord Bute and from the frustration which was the normal fate of Hanoverian heirs apparent. To understand the reign of George III, and the character of that unhappy monarch, it is necessary to look back to the years preceding his accession, to the Leicester House experience.

Leicester House was the residence of the Prince of Wales, and it gave its name to the political factions which formed around the heir apparent in the eighteenth century. In a period when English kings still enjoyed great power, it was natural that disgruntled politicians should look to the successor when thwarted by the incumbent. As one contemporary remarked, "in proportion as George II advanced in years, the Prince of Wales . . . acquired more influence."[1] The leaders of the Leicester House faction used this influence to sway numerous decisions, from routine matters of patronage to basic questions of national policy. It was, for example, alliance with Leicester House which helped bring William Pitt to power in 1757. And in another "most extraordinary" instance—the second British assault on St. Malo—a military expedition was planned entirely at Leicester House, without the knowledge or approval of any member of the government.

Even more important than this influence over the events of the late 1750's is the role of the Leicester House years in setting the stage for the reign of George III. For it was in the period from 1755 to 1760, while the prince was completely devoted to Lord Bute, that Prince George became prepared for the burdens of the crown. By 1760 he had become a man with a mission, convinced that corruption and moral decay were destroying England and that it was his duty to save her.

This pessimistic outlook was not original. All eighteenth century oppositions insisted that an evil cabal had captured

---

1. Louis Dutens, *Memoirs of a Traveller Now in Retirement* (London, 1806), I, 162.

the king and were using the royal prerogative to ruin the country. No one accepted this philosophy more wholeheartedly than Prince George and his "dearest friend," the Earl of Bute. The Leicester House group actually participated in opposition for less than two years, but even when the heir apparent was outwardly meek and submissive he remained convinced that his grandfather's ministers were wicked men, interested only in their own selfish concerns. Behind this bleak outlook stood Lord Bute, who admitted to the "meanest opinion" of politics and politicians. Few teachers have been more successful in inculcating their own prejudices in their pupils.

Young George's transformation is also partially explained by the discontent and anger which were normal parts of the Leicester House situation. Every Hanoverian Prince of Wales sought to escape from the control of the sovereign by participating in politics, and in each case this led to a one-sided battle where all the advantage lay with the king. Frustration and bitterness were the inevitable result, and this was never more true than in the 1750's.

Prince George anticipated great rewards when Pitt and the other Leicester House allies entered the ministry in 1757, but within two years all his hopes had turned to gall. Pitt soon quarrelled with Bute; the prince's request for permission to join the army was denied; Bute's military advisor, Lord George Sackville, was drummed out of the army for disobedience; and H. B. Legge, the prince's last ministerial ally, broke with Leicester House in 1759 because of an election dispute. To the prince and his favorite all of these incidents appeared as parts of a sinister plot, a plot designed to prevent them from saving Great Britain. Little wonder that George III ascended the throne convinced of the need for a drastic house-cleaning.

It is, then, in the petty and vindictive atmosphere of Leicester House that the bases for the reign of George III are to be found. Yet this Leicester House situation was not simply a repetition of well-worn cliches, as Romney Sedgwick and A. N. Newman would suggest. The ideas of George III may have been very similar to the professions of his father, Prince Frederick, or even to the Leicester House statements of the 1720's, but there is a crucial difference. George III was a moral zealot. Prince Frederick would appear ludicrous in the role of pious reformer; the same role suited George III perfectly. The key difference between the earlier Leicester House groups and George III and Bute was not their ideas, which were not original, but their moral self-righteousness, which was. Furthermore, it was this quality which clearly distinguishes George III from the first two Hanoverian monarchs and helps to explain the basic differences between his approach to kingship and theirs.

The present study represents an attempt to deal in depth with the ideas and activities of the Leicester House faction from 1755 to 1760, and to assess the impact of that milieu on the future George III. Such an attempt is overdue. No systematic effort has ever been made to investigate the Leicester House group of the 1750's and, despite the many writings in the area in recent years, no work based on original research dealing with the accession of George III has been published since 1939.

# GEORGE III AND LORD BUTE

ONE

# LORD BUTE AND PRINCE FREDERICK

The dominant figure at Leicester House in the late 1750's was John Stuart, third Earl of Bute. He was a handsome, well-educated Scotsman, a dilettante in the best eighteenth century sense, a student of art and literature, a passionate devotee of botany. But the favorite was also a proud man, acutely conscious of his own importance. Quick to take offence, he was slow to give up grudges. And, above all else, Bute was confident of his ability to mold a king and thereby shape a kingdom.

The earl was born in Edinburgh on May 11, 1713, the eldest son of the second earl and his wife, Lady Anne Campbell, the only daughter of the Duke of Argyll and Greenwich. His grandfather had been reluctant to accept either William III or the Act of Union of 1707, but Bute's father supported the Hanoverian succession and helped defeat the rebellion of 1715.[1] George I rewarded his loyalty by naming him a Lord of the Bedchamber, and the second earl also served as a Scottish Representative Peer until his death in 1723.

After his father's death the third earl was raised by his Campbell uncles, the Duke of Argyle and the Earl of Islay. The Campbells were the most powerful family in Scotland, and like the second Earl of Bute, they had sided decisively

---

1. On Bute's ancestry see Sir James Balfour Paul, ed., *The Scots Peerage* (Edinburgh, 1904–14), II, 284; John E. Reid, *History of the County of Bute* (Glasgow, 1864); R. Angus Downie, *Bute and the Cumbraes* (Glasgow, 1934).

with the new dynasty. Argyle, "a soldier from his cradle," had taken a leading part in suppressing the '15. Islay, who became Duke of Argyll after his brother's death in 1743, was "an able man of business," and the political manager of Scotland for George I and George II. Though their personalities were very different, both Argyle and Islay agreed that the Union of 1707 was the essential cornerstone for Scottish progress and that the Hanoverian succession must be preserved. These were the principles on which they brought up their young nephew.

Bute's education was designed to prepare him for the new opportunities which the Act of Union had opened to ambitious Scots. He was, in 1720, one of the first Scottish nobles to attend Eton, where William Pitt, George and Richard Grenville, and Horace Walpole were among his contemporaries.[2] He entered the University of Leyden in 1728, and took his degree four years later.[3] By 1732 Bute had become a stranger to Scotland, even his vacations from school having been spent at the English estate of his uncles.[4] By education and inclination the young earl was a member of the English aristocracy.

Bute broke still further from his Scottish background in 1736, when he was the first of his family to take an English wife. His bride, Mary, was the only daughter of the literary eccentric, Lady Mary Wortley Montagu, and her miserly husband, Mr. Wortley. Now that Bute was married, his uncles apparently decided that it was time to make provision for him, and in 1737 Lord Islay secured his election to fill a vacancy among the Scottish Representative Peers. In the same

2. Richard A. Austen Leigh, ed., *Eton College Register, 1698-1752* (Eton, 1927), pp. xvi-xvii, 57.
3. Edward Peacock, ed., *Index to English Speaking Students Who Have Graduated at Leyden University* (London, 1883), p. 16.
4. Lady Louisa Stuart, "Some Account of John, Duke of Argyll, and His Family," *Lady Louisa Stuart, Selections from Her Manuscripts*, ed. John Home (New York, 1899), p 3.

year he was appointed to a comfortable sinecure as one of the commissioners of police for Scotland, and in 1738 he was made a Knight of the Thistle.[5] As a personable and well connected young nobleman, Bute had every reason to assume that the future would provide still greater rewards.

In 1739, however, the young peer's orderly advancement suddenly stopped. Sir Robert Walpole's long reign as George II's chief minister was foundering on the issue of peace or war with Spain. Lord Islay stood with Walpole for peace; Argyle demanded war. Bute, forced for the first time to choose between his uncles, decided to back Argyle.[6] Despite Argyle's disaffection, Walpole won the crucial division on the Convention of Prado, and Bute and his uncle were forced into opposition. For Bute, it meant the end of his first political career. He spent the next six years in retirement on his native island, where it was cheaper to raise his rapidly growing family.

The seclusion of the Isle of Bute eventually began to pall, and the earl returned in 1745 to London, where he soon became the close friend of Frederick Lewis, Prince of Wales.[7] Frederick was an amiable and silly prince,[8] who never really matured. He loved to throw stones through aristocrats' windows, and he developed a pathological hatred for his parents so intense that when his wife was in labor he hustled her out of Hampton Court, so that the heir to the throne would not be born under George II's roof. The feeling was mutual, for as Lord Hervey said, "he had a father that abhorred him, a

5. *Gentleman's Magazine,* VII (1737), 574; VIII (1738), 381.
6. A. Bothwell to Bute, 3 March 1739, Bute MSS.
7. James McKelvey, "Lord Bute and George III: the Leicester House Years," doctoral dissertation (Northwestern, 1965), pp. 17–18.
8. The principal contemporary character sketches of Frederick were written by Lord Hervey and Horace Walpole, both of whom despised the prince: John, Lord Hervey, *Some Materials Towards Memoirs of the Reign of King George II,* ed Romney Sedgwick, I, 97–98; Horace Walpole, *Memoirs of the Reign of King George the Second* (London, 1846), I, 77; Horace Walpole, *Walpoliana* (London, 1819), p. 52.

mother that despised and neglected him, a sister that betrayed him." His mother, Queen Caroline, who constantly hoped for Frederick's early death, actually announced that she wished "the ground would open up this moment and sink the monster to the lowest hole in hell."[9]

Such family feuding was not unusual in the eighteenth century. Every Hanoverian monarch quarrelled with his heir. In part these quarrels resulted from the normal antipathy between generations which exists in all families, but more important were the political pressures that divided a royal father from his son. While the king enjoyed tremendous power and wealth, the heir was systematically excluded from any share in authority. The rulers all feared a contrast between their own lack of popularity and the public appeal of their eldest sons. George Augustus's success as regent in 1717 was one of the major reasons for the break between him and George I, and Frederick's warm welcome from the London crowds when he arrived in England in 1728 could hardly have pleased George II, whose subjects were, by that time, distinctly unenthusiastic about him.

This fear of the heir's popularity resulted in a refusal to permit him any sort of activity that might bring public approval. The popular enthusiasm resulting from George Augustus's valor at the battle of Oudenarde in 1708, ensured that no future heir apparent would be permitted to serve in the armed forces, though Frederick Lewis, George III, and George IV all requested to do so. On the last occasion, George IV's friends even raised the issue in Parliament.[10] Proposals for royal progresses by the princes, such as that made by Frederick in 1735, met with the same disapproval.[11]

9. Hervey, *Memoirs*, I, 309, 98; III, 681.
10. Roger Fulford, *George the Fourth*, rev. ed. (London, 1949), p. 62.
11. Betty Kemp, "Frederick, Prince of Wales," *Silver Renaissance*, ed. Alex Natan (London, 1961), p. 40.

Another cause of conflict was friction over money. The princes and their supporters claimed that £100,000 was included in the Civil List funds for the establishment of the Prince of Wales when he came of age. Each king, however, tried to keep his children under control by limiting their finances. George II received £100,000 when he was heir apparent, but he allowed his own son, Frederick, only £24,000, and then, grudgingly, £50,000 when the prince married. Frederick, feeling that he had been cheated, took the quarrel to Parliament in 1737, when a motion in his favor lost by only thirty votes in the House of Commons.[12]

Finally, among the major areas of altercation, there was the question of control over the heir apparent's children. George I, after he had evicted George Augustus and Princess Caroline from the royal palace, actually got a judicial opinion giving him control over his grandchildren. George II toyed with a similar idea, and tried to take Prince George away from his mother in 1756. The birth of a child was the immediate cause of the splits in the royal family in both 1717 and 1737.

The bitterness shown by the princes in their struggles with the kings is a reflection of the fact that the position of the heir apparent had many limitations. With the expectation of great power and wealth constantly before him, the prince nevertheless was expected to remain completely out of politics until the king's death, which was almost impossible in an era which still expected royalty to rule as well as reign. After the regency of 1717, there was never any question of a Prince of Wales serving an apprenticeship in a government position. He was expected to spend his time in obedient idleness. Little wonder that the princes often expressed ill-disguised wishes for the death of the monarch.

Such antagonisms between father and son are not restricted

---

12. This issue reappeared in the 1780's, when George III was accused of stinginess in providing for his heir.

to England or to the eighteenth century. Peter the Great beheaded his eldest son and Frederick William I of Prussia imprisoned his heir. In the nineteenth century the crown princes of both Austria and Germany championed political programs opposite to those of their fathers. But it was only in Britain, and only in the period from the Glorious Revolution to the Reform Act of 1832, that there was a readily available method by which the prince could apply pressure on his royal father with relatively little fear of drastic reprisals. This was through alliance with the opposition to the king's ministers in Parliament.

The concept of "the king's loyal opposition" had yet to evolve, and opposition to the ministry was considered perilously close to Jacobitism. Thus the leaders of a parliamentary opposition were always pleased to secure the aid of the Prince of Wales, whose participation must necessarily destroy any claim that they were disguised Jacobites. The princes, in turn, subscribed to the policies of the opposition, and occasionally even came to believe in its propositions.

In the 1720's Lord Bolingbroke presented the first coherent statement of the opposition philosophy. Sir Robert Walpole, he claimed, was the very epitome of faction. The minister had disgraced his opponents by labelling them as Jacobites, and thereby succeeded in capturing the crown and its prerogatives. Walpole, according to Bolingbroke, maintained himself in power only by the use of "corruption" on an unprecedented scale. What was needed was the destruction of meaningless party distinctions, and the formation of a new, "patriot," policy, based on rule by men of good will, who would use the royal prerogative for the benefit of all Englishmen, rather than for the personal aggrandizement of the favored few. Obstructing the king's government was thus a temporary necessity, unfortunate because it appeared to signify opposition to the king, but actually designed to save both king and nation from their bondage to the unscrupulous Walpole and his cohorts.

Ideas alone could not make a successful opposition. Numbers and unity were both essential. The former was supplied by the "country gentlemen," the independent members, who frequently represented county seats, and who served both their country and their locality through a sense of duty. They had little interest in the political struggles of the day, but they were concerned about the state of the country. The country gentlemen's much boasted independence made them extremely difficult to forge into an effective force, however. When Dodington suggested to Lord Chesterfield that it would be wise to have a meeting of all opposition supporters before the opening of the parliamentary session of 1741, Chesterfield replied that he had been trying to do just that for seven years, but that "fox-hunting, gardening, planting or indifference," had "always kept our people in the country, till the very day before the meeting of the parliament."[13]

Despite their unreliability, much of the program supported by the opposition was designed to attract the country gentlemen. When Prince Frederick bargained with them in 1748, he promised on his accession to "abolish for the future all distinction of party," to exclude low ranking military officers from Parliament, to increase the militia, to fight corruption, and to limit the Civil List to £800,000.[14] All of these "reforms" were close to the hearts of the country gentlemen.

Even if the independent members could be effectively mustered, as they were at the downfall of Walpole in 1742, other problems remained for the opposition. All eighteenth century oppositions were collections of small factions. This was equal-

13. Chesterfield to George Dodington, 8 September 1741, W. Coxe, *Memoirs of the Life and Administration of Sir Robert Walpole* (London, 1798), III, 579.
14. "Proposal Carried from H.R.H. by Lord Talbot and Sir Francis Dashwood to ———. February 8, 1748," *Correspondence of John, Fourth Duke of Bedford*, ed. Lord John Russell (London, 1842–46), I, 320–22.

ly true of the administration, but with the important difference that the alliance of factions in power was able to tie its disparate elements together through the application of patronage. The opposition could never match government largesse, but it could offer the hope of seizing the sources of government affluence. This was the one thing that held oppositions together—the prospect of overturning the government. The more remote this possibility, the less cohesive the party.

In a normal parliamentary session there was little to excite passion. It was when a strong issue arose, such as excise taxes or subsidy treaties, that the opposition had its best opportunity. Passive M.P.'s could then be stirred to action, the country gentlemen might remain until the end of the session, and the alarmed ministers might make a fatal blunder. In other, quieter, periods the best the opposition leaders could do was to bide their time and try to hold the nucleus of a political force together.

What was the position of the Prince of Wales in all this? It has already been mentioned that his adherance to the opposition destroyed the taint of Jacobitism. The prince also supplied a rallying point, a national figure, in a way that men like Pulteney or Carteret could not. The prince became the figurehead of the opposition whenever he joined it.

The prince also had another role. He was, in his own right, a political leader of considerable importance. In an age where politicians were often judged by how many votes they controlled in Parliament, the Prince of Wales had one of the largest individual followings. His group was very similar to the Court or Treasury "party" in that it was based on patronage. It was far smaller than the force the ministers could provide, but it was one of the most considerable factions in Parliament, and it had an advantage over many other groups because it was held together by the disciplinary power of greed. The best example is to be found in the household of

Prince Frederick. At the time of his death in 1751, the prince's establishment included four peers, twenty-eight members of Parliament, and close relatives of five other members.[15] There is no question that the prince used these appointments to build a compact and loyal political following.

Furthermore, the prince would, presumably, be king, and his followers lived with the expectation of rich rewards yet to come. This prospect of future benefits is what has become known as the "reversionary interest."[16] While the reversionary interest was never a matter of precise calculation, the Prince of Wales could promise his supporters great things upon his accession. As Robert Walpole said to Queen Caroline in 1737, when Frederick went over to the opposition: "your son makes interest by promising what yet is not in his power."[17] It was also true, Lord Chesterfield pointed out, that the heir's pledges became more appealing "as the King grows older."[18]

The prestige and the personal following of the Prince of Wales enabled him to play a leading role whenever he joined the opposition. The prince, however, was rarely *the* leader. The "Leicester House oppositions" were usually a conjunction of the prince and his adherents with the various groups that were already opposing the ministry. There was never a complete amalgamation into a single, unified, opposition party. The objectives of the various groups always differed; each sought to preserve its own identity and to forward its own interests. The results of opposition, therefore, were never equally satisfactory to all participants.

Most of the politicians in the opposition, as opposed to the

15. A. N. Newman, "The Political Patronage of Frederick Lewis, Prince of Wales," *The Historical Journal*, I (1958), 74.
16. For the best discussions of the reversionary interest see Lewis Namier, *England in the Age of the American Revolution*, 2nd ed. (London, 1961), pp. 53–57; Romney Sedgwick, ed., *Letters from George III to Lord Bute, 1756–1766* (London, 1939), pp. xi–xix; Hervey, *Memoirs*, I, xxxi *et seq.*
17. Hervey, *Memoirs*, III, 702.
18. Chesterfield to Solomon Dayrolles, 25 April 1749, *The Letters of Lord Chesterfield*, ed. Bonamy Dobree (London, 1932), IV, 1333.

country gentlemen, were actively seeking office. They felt that the ministry was ignoring or undervaluing their talents, and that the best way to demonstrate this was to show their nuisance value. A successful opposition policy, from their point of view, was one which brought them into the government. The prince, on the other hand, usually sought redress of an immediate grievance—an increase in his allowance, for example—and he wanted to play a larger role in national affairs. As Prince Frederick pointed out when he went into opposition in 1737, "by showing I have weight enough to make my father change his administration, [I] shall make a much better figure than I can do by being quiet."[19]

While a politician could obviously benefit from being a nuisance, as William Pitt proved, the value of this for the prince was highly questionable. The prince usually gained the immediate concession he wanted as the price the king was willing to pay for his heir's withdrawal from opposition. The future George II, on his reconciliation with his father in 1720, had the social ban lifted which had kept all but the bravest friends from his door; Frederick succeeded in getting his allowance raised; George III remained with his mother and had Lord Bute appointed his Groom of the Stole. But no prince achieved his larger goal of an increased role in politics. If the opposition were successful, its leaders would be taken into office, where they would become the king's servants, not the prince's. Some of them might sincerely try to maintain their ties with the heir, but this generally proved impossible, and most of the prince's colleagues soon forgot their benefactor.[20] The prince thus ceased to be the leader of a powerful political combination and returned to his role as a distinctly subordinate member of the royal family.

19. Hervey, *Memoirs*, III, 704.
20. For a prophetic statement by Dodington on this subject, see his "Memorial" to Frederick: George Bubb Dodington, *The Diary of the Late George Bubb Dodington*, ed. Henry Penruddocke Wyndham, 4th ed. (London, 1823), p. 426.

Frederick had already gone through one complete cycle of opposition before he met Bute. In 1747 Frederick launched his second major effort to overthrow his father's ministry. Bute's role in Frederick's entourage, however, does not appear to have been political. He was not even a member of the House of Lords, and there is no evidence that he was ever called on by Frederick to aid his cause in Scotland. Instead, Bute became one of the leaders in the social activities of the prince's residences at Leicester House and Richmond Lodge, and in October, 1750, he was named one of Frederick's Lords of the Bedchamber.[21] His mother-in-law wrote Bute that she wished him "joy of his place," but that she was "glad you do not too much found hopes on things of so much uncertainty."[22]

There was more uncertainty than Lady Mary or anyone else could have anticipated, for, five months later, Prince Frederick died and the masterless Lord of the Bedchamber returned to political obscurity.

---

21. *Gentleman's Magazine*, XX (1750), 477.
22. Lady Mary to the Countess of Bute, [17 October 1750], in W. Moy Thomas, ed., *The Letters and Works of Lady Mary Wortley Montagu*, 3rd ed. (London, 1861), II, 200.

TWO

## THE EMERGENCE OF A NEW LEICESTER HOUSE FACTION

Prince Frederick's widow lost no time in establishing a new direction at Leicester House. After burning her husband's papers, Princess Augusta removed her support from the opposition and quickly came to terms with George II.[1]

The Dowager Princess of Wales was a quiet, homely woman, notable mainly for her "inoffensive good sense."[2] During her husband's lifetime she had remained consistently in the background, though she had disapproved of many of his more foolhardy actions, particularly when they aggravated the feud with his parents.[3] Pregnant when Frederick died, Princess Augusta was necessarily concerned for the welfare of her numerous children. She knew the opposition could do nothing for them, so she turned back to the king. George II was equally ready to end the conflict in the royal family, and they soon agreed on an establishment for the princess and the young princes. Augusta received an allowance of £50,000 a year—a very generous sum for the miserly king—and was named regent, in case George II should die before his grandson came of age.

In return for these favors, the king's chief ministers, Henry Pelham and his brother, the Duke of Newcastle, were given the privilege of staffing the Prince of Wales' establishment. The three principal officers were all closely associated with

1. Walpole, *George II*, I, 77.
2. *Ibid.*, I, 76.
3. Hervey, *Memoirs*, III, 807.

the Pelhams. The governor, Lord Harcourt, was a nondescript gentleman, "civil and sheepish," "who wanted a governor himself."[4] The preceptor, or chief tutor, was Bishop Hayter, whom George III later described as an "intriguing, unworthy man, more fitted to be a Jesuit than an English bishop."[5] The most substantial of the men placed about the young prince was the subgovernor, Andrew Stone, brother of the Archbishop of Armagh and Newcastle's confidant and former private secretary. With such an entourage the Pelhams anticipated that the Prince of Wales would be brought up a good Whig and continue their power into the next reign.

For the next four years Princess Augusta remained the picture of discretion. There was a minor flurry of excitement at Leicester House in 1752, when Harcourt and Hayter accused Stone and two of his colleagues of Jacobitism, but the charges were proven baseless.[6] Augusta was pleased with the handling of this scandal in the House of Lords, and she attributed this success to George II. "It is remarkable," Bubb Dodington wrote in his diary, "that this is the first time, that I ever heard her speak favorably of the King."[7] The princess soon reverted to "her usual dislike of the King,"[8] but she knew enough to conceal this dislike in public, for her security, and that of her children, depended on the caprice of the monarch.[9]

The princess's prudent friendship extended not only to the king, but also to his ministers, and especially to the Duke

4. Walpole, *George II*, I, 74.
5. Leveson Vernon Harcourt, ed., *The Diaries and Correspondence of the Right Hon. George Rose* (London, 1860), II, 188; William Coxe, *Memoirs of the Administration of the Right Honourable Henry Pelham* (London, 1829), II, 167.
6. Earl of Ilchester, *Henry Fox, First Lord Holland* (London, 1920), I, App. A, 361–62; for the best description of this affair see Sedgwick, *Letters from George III*, pp. xxi–xxviii.
7. Dodington, *Diary*, pp. 207–8.
8. *Ibid.*, p. 257.
9. William, Earl of Shelburne, "Autobiography," in Lord Fitzmaurice, *Life of William, Earl of Shelburne*, 2nd ed., 2 vols. (London, 1912), I, 54; James, Earl Waldegrave, *Memoirs from 1754 to 1758* (London, 1821), pp. 36–37.

of Newcastle. Stone faithfully reported the good tidings to the duke: "The Princess of Wales . . . always speaks of Your Grace with great regard, & in the most gracious manner."[10] When a minor functionary in the prince's household died, the princess hastened to name one of the Duchess of Newcastle's servants to the vacancy.[11] Much more important for Newcastle's peace of mind was the complete absence of political activity at Leicester House. After Frederick's death, the princess refused to continue the electoral interest he had painfully built up in Grampound and several other boroughs,[12] and in at least one instance intervened to help defeat an old adherent of her late husband.[13]

One important reason for the princess's cooperation with the king and Newcastle was yet another rift in the royal family, this time between Augusta and her brother-in-law, the Duke of Cumberland, the king's favorite son. Cumberland was captain-general of the British army and had a considerable following in Parliament, headed by Henry Fox and the Duke of Bedford. It was widely believed that he sought to ascend the throne, and even Lord Waldegrave, one of the "Butcher's" best friends, suspected that Cumberland might try to overturn a regency.[14] Certainly the princess viewed him as the chief threat to her security.

So long as Cumberland was not appointed regent and the Pelhams had a firm grip on power, Leicester House was apprehensive, but not unduly alarmed. After Henry Pelham died on March 6, 1754, however, the situation changed abruptly. In the confusion following his death, the princess dowager began to wonder whether Dodington had been right when he

10. Stone to Newcastle, 1 May 1752, B.M. Add. MS. 32,727, f. 59.
11. Stone to Newcastle, 17 July 1752, B.M. Add. MS. 32,728, ff. 292–93.
12. Robert Andrews to Newcastle, 14 February 1756, B.M. Add. MS. 32,862, f. 490.
13. James Cresset to Newcastle, 16 April 1754, B.M. Add. MS. 32,735, f. 96.
14. Waldegrave, *Memoirs*, pp. 23–24.

## A NEW LEICESTER HOUSE FACTION

had repeatedly urged her to safeguard her position by forming a political party of her own.[15]

On the death of his brother, the principal power in the ministry fell into the shaky hands of the Duke of Newcastle, who was immediately faced with a major problem. Someone would have to take Pelham's place as the ministerial leader in the House of Commons. The two prime candidates were already in office, Fox as secretary-at-war, Pitt as paymaster general, but both clearly felt destined for greater things. Unless one or the other of them were won over to the administration, wide breaches might well begin to appear in the parliamentary majority Newcastle had worked so hard to build.

The ministry had good reasons for avoiding both Pitt and Fox. Fox was Cumberland's chief representative, and as such was distrusted by both Newcastle and Leicester House. Pitt had a still more formidable handicap—George II hated him for remarks he had made in Parliament during the last Leicester House opposition. After an attempted deal with Fox collapsed, it was decided to delay a decision by naming Sir Thomas Robinson secretary of state and leader in the Commons. This was obviously a stopgap measure; Robinson had never spoken in debate during his six years in Parliament. He was no match for the guile of Fox or for the oratory of Pitt, if either should oppose the government's measures.

The temporary nature of this arrangement became clear when the new session of Parliament opened in November. Fox and Pitt buried their personal differences and cooperated in constant harassment of the ministry. This "guarded opposition" soon had Newcastle thoroughly frightened, and the result was a new bargain with Fox, who, while remaining secretary-at-war, was elevated to cabinet rank. In return for promises of future benefits, Fox promised to support the government's measures.

15. Dodington, *Diary*, pp. 146–47, and *passim*.

The remainder of the parliamentary session passed quietly, and no further problems arose until April, 1755, when, with war with France obviously approaching, George II insisted on leaving for Hanover, and Cumberland was unexpectedly named president of the Regency Council for the king's stay abroad. This, combined with Fox's recent promotion, threw Leicester House into a panic. The spectre of military dictatorship, long a nagging suspicion, now seemed a real possibility.

It was at this juncture, with Augusta distressed by the rise of Cumberland and with Pitt excluded from the ministry, that the Earl of Bute reappeared in the counsels of Leicester House.[16] Bute had slipped into obscurity after the death of Prince Frederick, but he had retained an interest in public affairs. When his good friend, Gilbert Elliot, wrote from Edinburgh that he had decided that English politics were "not very wicked, tho' extremely frivolous. Little competitions, womanish rivalship, & narrow views, & an unconcern for the publick, seem to be the greatest of our political vices,"[17] Bute replied that he could not agree:

> I rejoice in that tranquillity that reigns in Your breast; how different from the gloomy apprehensions that arise in Mine; can you really think there is occasion to go to Tacitus & Davila for perfidy dissimulation &c; no no wee have them here, & as strongly rooted as ever they were in any age . . .

Furthermore, Bute had plans for dealing with the "perfidy" that had so degraded Britain. Newcastle's "timidity" had led him to bring Fox into the cabinet and propose Cumberland for regent; "it has altogether an ugly look." Nonetheless,

---

16. Bute was in considerable favor with Augusta by the summer of 1755: Sir George Lee to [Bute], 28 July 1755, B.M. Add. MS. 5726, D, f. 198, B, f. 55.
17. Gilbert Elliot to Bute, 18 April 1755, Bute MSS.

Bute wrote, "some good may . . . spring from this black cloud, & I think I see it dawn already." Next year the Prince of Wales will be of age, and "I think tis likely a Strong Party will be form'd." If Pitt can be persuaded to join, "a point I have much at heart," then both Fox and Newcastle will regret their actions. Bute closed his letter with a cryptic prediction: "I think, a few days will produce, some thing more Certain."[18]

It soon became apparent what Bute meant by this last statement. "In consequence of a conversation" between Bute and Pitt in the early days of May, the princess, Pitt, and Sir George Lee met on May 5 at Bute's house in South Audley Street, where Pitt declared to Augusta his desire "to support her & preserve the independence of the Prince, whenever he should come to the Crown." Pitt added, however, that his friends feared that the princess was under the influence of Stone and Newcastle, and "this gave the true constitutional Whigs who acted upon Revolution principles great alarm." Augusta assured him that she was not under the domination of Newcastle or anyone else, but "that she would always contenance those the King employed, & should never oppose the King's measures."[19]

On the basis of this opening, another meeting was held at Bute's house on the following night, with Pitt, Lee, and Bute present. Bute and Lee "declared a desire of cementing friendship," and Pitt said that he was honored and "would do all he could to connect people" with the Princess of Wales, "that she might have a strong party if any thing should happen." Lee assured Pitt that there was no formal connection between Leicester House and Newcastle, and that the princess had been very unhappy with Newcastle's actions during the past winter,

18. Bute to Elliot, 27 April 1755, Minto MSS, National Library of Scotland.
19. Sir George Lee, "Memorandum of what passed between the Princess, Sr. George, Mr. Pitt, and Ld. Bute, upon the Coalition, 1755," in H. W. Smyth, *Aedes Hartwellianae, or Notices of the Manor and Mansion of Hartwell*, Addenda (London, 1864), p. 146.

"for he had thrown the game into Mr. Fox's hand." Pitt wanted a specific commitment that Newcastle would not become a minister in a new reign, but Lee said that he did not have authority to make such a promise. They adjourned until the next day, when Bute told Pitt that the princess reaffirmed her lack of connection with Newcastle, but that she did not think it proper to declare herself "positively" against anyone.[20]

The alliance between Pitt and Leicester House was thus concluded. "We both declared," wrote Lee, that "this was a defensive treaty only to connect people together, but did not bind us to hostility agst any person, or to opposition to the King's measures."[21] Both parties soon affirmed their good faith. On May 7, the princess dowager told Dodington that "she desired it might be understood, that her house had no communication with Newcastle House."[22] Pitt, two days later, met Fox at Lord Hillsborough's and declared that their cooperation was at an end.[23] The negotiations were then broadened to include Pitt's "friends."[24] After several meetings between Bute and the leaders of the Grenville "cousinhood" the more formal terms of alliance were completed.[25]

At the same time Bute was trying to bring Pitt into the fold, he was also attempting to preserve as much of the old Leicester House party as possible. This was not easy. The two major politicians still nominally attached to the princess, Lee and Lord Egmont, were notoriously jealous of each other, and

20. *Ibid.*, p. 147.
21. *Ibid.*
22. Dodington, *Diary*, p. 284.
23. *Ibid.*, pp. 284–85; Fox to Lord Hartington, 13 May 1755, in Waldegrave, *Memoirs*, App., p. 155.
24. George Grenville, "Mr. Grenville's Narrative," in William J. Smith, ed., *The Grenville Papers* (London, 1852–53), I, 432–33; George F. S. Elliot, *The Border Elliots and the Family of Minto* (Edinburgh, 1897), p. 342; for a somewhat different version see Shelburne, "Autobiography," I, 54.
25. The precise terms are unknown. For what Pitt thought they were five years later, see Gilbert Elliot's Memorandum on a conversation with Pitt [early May, 1760], Minto MSS, National Library of Scotland, pub. in slightly different form in Namier, *England*, pp. 105–7.

neither liked the prospect of being subordinated to Pitt. Bute, however, was able to bring about a temporary settlement, and a second meeting between Pitt and Augusta put the final approval to the new arrangements.[26]

The new allies managed to hide their agreement for some time,[27] and even when the alliance became known it was universally believed to be between Pitt and Egmont.[28] Bute remained in the background. It was clear, however, that he had by this time become Augusta's closest adviser. The princess felt that Bute was the only one of her husband's former associates who had always remained loyal to her,[29] and when she thought herself obliged to form a party, it was to Bute that she naturally turned.

This new Leicester House opposition did not, at first, seem a very important addition to the political scene. It included several able politicians, most notably Pitt, the leading orator in an age when speeches could still influence votes in Parliament. Egmont, Lee, Elliot, George Grenville, and Lord Temple were all more than competent. No matter how imposing the leadership might be, however, the group was sadly deficient in numbers. The only voting strength in the House of Commons that they could hope to marshal was the country gentlemen, a group described by Horace Walpole as "about a hundred of the silentest and most impotent votes."[30]

Against the meager forces of Leicester House was gathered Newcastle's greatest majority, the Parliament elected in 1754. This new House of Commons represented the culmination of almost half a century of assiduous borough nurturing by

26. Bute to Pitt, 11 [May 1755], PRO 30/8/24, f. 10.
27. See McKelvey, "Bute and George III," pp. 51–52.
28. Stone to Newcastle, [24 June 1755], B.M. Add. MS. 32,856, f. 165; Fox to Lord Hartington, 16 July 1755, in Waldegrave, *Memoirs*, App., p. 161.
29. Elliot Memorandum, Minto MSS, National Library of Scotland, M6, no. 1; Francis Bickley, ed., *The Diaries of Sylvester Douglas, Lord Glenbervie* (London, 1928), II, 10.
30. Walpole, *George II*, II, 12.

the duke, and nothing but the most astounding of issues could threaten Newcastle's vast, mute following.

This issue was notably lacking. The men gathered under the standard of Leicester House could agree only on their mutual dislike of the present ministry. Augusta thought "it was of infinite consequence how a young reign began"; and she therefore wanted a government more obviously favorable to the Prince of Wales.[31] Pitt felt that he had been consigned too long to the political wilderness; like other politicians before him he wanted to use Leicester House as a lever to force himself upon an unwilling king. Egmont and Lee had both relished "reversions" for many years, but Egmont was willing to cooperate with anyone who would supply him with the one thing he wanted above all else, an English peerage. Bute, Elliot, and a few others seem to have taken the old Leicester House slogans seriously. They really believed that England was on the brink of ruin because of the machinations of the Whig oligarchs and could only be saved by a glorious new reign. All of the members of the new coalition desired to gain concessions from the king and his ministers by opposing the government. For this blackmail to succeed, however, the opposition had to pose a real threat to the administration's hold on Parliament, and this was impossible unless something destroyed public lethargy. George II, happily summering in Hanover, soon did just that, and, in addition, he made a proposal which confirmed Princess Augusta in her feeling that political support was necessary for the security of her family.

The king, much taken with the elder daughter of the Duchess of Brunswick Wolfenbüttel, had decided that she would make an excellent wife for the young Prince of Wales. Aside from the undeniable charms of the princess, there were also political advantages to such a match. The duchess was Frederick the Great's sister, and Hanover was extremely vulnerable

31. Waldegrave, *Memoirs*, p. 40.

to attack from Prussia. Furthermore, the old king wanted to see his grandson married before he died, so that Augusta "should have no temptation to do a job for her relations, by marrying her son to one of the Saxe Gotha family."[32] Augusta was horrified. According to Walpole, the news of the king's plans "at once unhinged all the circumspection and prudence of the Princess."[33]

Augusta was not completely "unhinged"; she remained diplomatic when Stone mentioned the proposed marriage to her, but despite her restraint Stone emerged from the interview convinced that she found the idea "very disagreeable."[34] Augusta disliked the bride's mother, and she may also have feared losing control over her son to an attractive wife. She soon convinced the Prince of Wales that the marriage was an evil plot conceived by his grandfather, who was "marrying him off for the interests of Hanover," a most detestable reason in the eyes of Leicester House.[35] Young George's hatred of the old king probably dates from this incident. Certainly it determined Augusta on the necessity of moving ahead with her plans for opposition. By the middle of August, Pitt's friends were being treated with ostentatious good will at Leicester House and Kew. At the same time, however, the princess remained convinced of the need for avoiding an outright break with the king,[36] for she had seen the results of such behavior by her husband. She would quarrel with his ministers, but not directly with her father-in-law.

Meanwhile the opposition was greatly strengthened by further news from Germany. George II, fearing that his beloved Hanover would be the first victim in the impending war between England and France, negotiated treaties on his

32. *Ibid.*
33. Walpole, *George II*, II, 36.
34. Stone to Newcastle, 18 August 1755, B.M. Add. MS. 32,858, f. 197.
35. Dodington, *Diary*, p. 317; Waldegrave, *Memoirs*, pp. 40–41.
36. Dodington, *Diary*, p. 284.

own initiative with Hesse Cassel and Russia, calling for those states to supply troops in return for English subsidies. Subsidy treaties had been a staple part of British foreign policy since the time of William III, but they were never popular in England. This was particularly true at Leicester House, where Hanover was despised and the subsidies were viewed solely as English payments for Hanoverian security. Attacks on subsidy treaties had been a key feature of the opposition in the 1740's, and it soon became apparent that this was once again to be the case.

Now that they had a popular issue, the leaders of the Leicester House party began to organize their strength for the coming parliamentary session. Much of their time was spent in seeking new adherents. Negotiations were opened with many of the leading politicians of the day, including the Townshends, the Duke of Bedford, the Duke of Devonshire, and Lord Halifax. Several of these men professed themselves to be in agreement with the aims of the opposition, but they hesitated to pit themselves against Newcastle. At one point Bute seems to have even entertained hopes of weaning his uncle, the Duke of Argyll, away from the ministry.[37] Though this came to nothing, a few lesser figures did attach themselves to the princess, and the summer produced one notable convert from within the ministry itself.

H. B. Legge, the chancellor of the Exchequer, had long felt mistreated by the head of his department, the Duke of Newcastle. Approached by Pitt, Legge listened eagerly to his overtures. Pitt introduced him to Bute, and a plan was laid for Legge to detach himself from the administration in a manner with great propaganda value.[38] The warrant for the first payment on the Hessian subsidy was soon to come before the Treasury Board. What better way could be found for Legge

37. Gilbert Elliot to Bute, 31 August 1755, Bute MSS.
38. Legge to Bute, 7 August 1755, Bute MSS.

to declare his independence from Newcastle than for him to decline to sign the warrant on the grounds that it was unconstitutional, since the treaty had not been approved by Parliament? Legge duly "refused his hand to the warrant" and became the most popular man in London.[39] He had traded the profits of the Exchequer for the expectation of the same office in the next reign.[40] As Newcastle cast about for a new chancellor, Legge became one of the most active members of the opposition. Like Pitt before him, Legge had cut his ties with the ministry in the most public of fashions, and had then been accepted by Leicester House. In both cases, the gesture seems to have been part of the price for alliance.

With the addition of Legge, there existed by late summer the nucleus of a strong opposition. Although the nature of this new party came to be known only gradually, the general outline was already clear. This was enough to terrify Newcastle, who reacted in a predictable fashion. He sought to emasculate this new threat by luring the chief members of the opposition over to the ministerial side, with specific positions if necessary, but even more with tantalizing prospects for the future.

The key to the situation was Pitt. Without him the others would simply be another band of disgruntled politicians. Newcastle began his maneuvers by gaining the king's reluctant permission to bargain with Pitt and Egmont.[41] Unfortunately for Newcastle, he had no idea of the scope of Pitt's ambition. The duke was prepared to offer Pitt the same terms that had succeeded with Fox—a seat in the Cabinet Council and the possibility of a later promotion to secretary of state—but only if Pitt cooperated wholeheartedly with the administration.

39. [Richard Glover], *Memoirs of a Celebrated Literary and Political Character* (London, 1813), pp. 46–47.
40. "Mr. Grenville's Narrative," I, 434.
41. Newcastle to Holdernesse, 11 July 1755, B.M. Egerton MS. 3429, ff. 78–81; Holdernesse to Newcastle, 20 July 1755, B.M. Egerton MS. 3429, f. 129.

Pitt insisted on a policy making appointment, not merely a spokesman's role, and this Newcastle refused to consider.

The hand of Leicester House is obvious in all of these negotiations during the late summer of 1755. Newcastle, in his usual cautious way, had authorized Stone to sound out the princess before dealing openly with Pitt and Egmont. Stone reported that Augusta was "very much pleased" with Newcastle's plans, though she was not "acquainted" with Pitt's "disposition or intention."[42] It is doubtful that she was actually so enthusiastic. The policy of Leicester House was one of deliberate obscurity. When Newcastle saw Egmont on August 26, he received no definite answers to his questions, though he emerged with a feeling of satisfaction.[43] Egmont gave the impression that, while he did not approve of what was going on at Leicester House, he did not want to come into office alone.

Actually, Egmont was bitter over losing his prime position with the princess to Bute and Pitt, and was thus the weakest link in the opposition forces. He was not yet willing to commit himself finally to Newcastle, however, and at the end of August, 1755, he was still included in the consultations of the opposition leaders.[44] By fall, however, his attempts to please both the duke and the princess had resulted in his alienation from both, and from any real prospect of political power. Sir George Lee was even more elusive. He had known of the duke's plan to make him chancellor of the Exchequer for at least a year and had appeared to be pleased by the idea.[45] Now, with no warning to his prospective benefactor, Lee announced his opposition to the subsidy treaties.[46]

42. Stone to Newcastle, 18 August 1755, B.M. Add. MS. 32,858, f. 197.
43. Newcastle to Stone, Tuesday [26 August 1755], B.M. Add. MS. 32,858, ff. 294-95.
44. Bute to Pitt, 31 August [1755], PRO 30/8/24, f. 325.
45. Thad W. Riker, *Henry Fox, First Lord Holland* (Oxford, 1911), I, 311.
46. Newcastle to Hardwicke, 22 August 1755, B.M. Add. MS. 32,858, f. 241.

Pitt and the Grenvilles were concerned primarily with the forthcoming opening of Parliament. The failure of the government's foreign policy had given them increased hope for a successful opposition. While war with France had seemed inevitable ever since Colonel Washington's abortive attack on the French in the summer of 1754, the Newcastle ministry had hoped to restrict the hostilities to America. By the summer of 1755, however, it was clear that this policy had failed. Braddock's defeat and Boscawen's subsequent attack on the French fleet had opened the floodgates, and a general war appeared imminent.

Both countries began looking for allies, and it was at this point that George II negotiated the subsidy treaties with Hesse Cassel and Russia. To Pitt and his friends it seemed apparent that the king and Newcastle were once again thinking in terms of a continental war, where the first priority would be the safety of Hanover. Fear of another Treaty of Aix la Chapelle, another surrender of British gains for Hanoverian security, inflamed public opinion. War with France was popular, but Hanover was universally disliked in England. The Archbishop of Canterbury was exaggerating when he told Newcastle that the country was in an uproar comparable to the hysteria of 1745,[47] but Pitt knew that the public was on his side when he demanded an all out colonial and naval war.

The administration leaders, worried by the strength which the war would give to the opposition, began looking for weaknesses among their opponents. Since Bute's influence at Leicester House was gradually becoming known, Hardwicke suggested to Newcastle on September 29, that he should "try to get my Lord Bute, who has credit there, & undoubtedly would be glad of something for himself."[48] Newcastle broached

47. Basil Williams, *The Life of William Pitt, Earl of Chatham* (London, 1913), I, 262.
48. Hardwicke to Newcastle, 29 September 1755, B.M. Add. MS. 32,859, f. 265.

the idea of Bute to George II, who advised that Argyll be employed "to get" the earl for the administration.[49] Nothing came of this proposal in 1755, and when the idea was revived in the following year circumstances were very different.

As the real test for the opposition approached, the pretence surrounding the formation of the new alliance was dropped. In the weeks before the opening of Parliament, Pitt and his followers were given every distinction at Leicester House. Henry Fox, on October 28, reported that "at no time did the late Prince of Wales lay his designs before his drawing-room, or mark them more strongly than she and her children did hers . . . Pitt acted, and was treated as the Minister there as much as Sr. R. Walpole in Queen Caroline's" time.[50] Bute "was distinguished by the most particular marks of favor and confidence." At the same time the prince and princess took "that kind of notice of the king's principal servants which at court is called *rumping*."[51]

Even though Augusta's support of the opposition was obvious to all, she still sought to avoid an open break with the king. George II had learned of his daughter-in-law's behavior be-before he returned to England in the fall of 1755,[52] but, despite his hatred for Pitt, the king did not rush into the violent fury so feared by Newcastle. George II did make one disastrous attempt at personal intervention, when he sought to detach the young prince from his mother's domination by reasoning with him, but the conversation proved a complete failure, with the prince pretending not to understand his grandfather.[53] The princess dowager, for her part, emphasized that

49. Newcastle to Hardwicke, 18 October 1755, B.M. Add. MS. 32,860, ff. 89–90.
50. Fox to Hartington, 28 October 1755, in W. M. Torrens, *History of Cabinets from the Union with Scotland* (London, 1894), II, 238–39.
51. Waldegrave, *Memoirs*, p. 50.
52. Holdernesse to Newcastle, 13 September 1755, B.M. Egerton MS. 3429, ff. 309–11.
53. Newcastle to Hardwicke, 18 October 1755, B.M. Add. MS. 35,415, ff. 108–13.

anyone who misrepresented her to the king would be her enemy.[54] She assured Cresset, knowing that he would pass it on to Newcastle, "that She would *never* oppose the King, but She would be Tranquille, & would do nothing, nor speak to any Body, nor Influence any of Her Servants one way, or Other."[55] Augusta's implication that she had no control over the political activities of her associates was, of course, nonsense. She was still trying to gain advantages from an opposition without suffering the results which had befallen her husband.

Both ministry and opposition maintained a high pitch of recruitment right up to the November 13 meeting of Parliament. As late as November 3, Bute and Pitt still hoped for such important converts as the Dukes of Devonshire and Bedford.[56] The laurels, however, went to Newcastle. Bubb Dodington, who had been eagerly mapping strategy with Pitt in September announced his adherence to the ministry in October.[57] His reward was the Treasurership of the Navy, the salve for his conscience the right to oppose the subsidies in the House of Commons.

Newcastle was thus able to face the parliamentary opening more cheerfully than was normal for him. As late as October 12, he had written Hardwicke that "Every Body is full of the Behaviour of Leicester House, and it operates more than All other Considerations put together."[58] After drawing up "for" and "against" lists, however, Newcastle reported to the lord chancellor that "our Line of Battle in the House of Commons

54. [Stone] to Newcastle, [16 September 1755], B.M. Add. MS. 32,859, f. 104.
55. Newcastle to Hardwicke, 28 September 1755 ,B.M. Add. MS. 35,415, ff. 80–81.
56. Pitt to Bute, Monday 12 at night [2 November 1755], Bute MSS, in Romney Sedgwick, ed., "Letters from William Pitt to Lord Bute," *Essays Presented to Sir Lewis Namier*, ed. Richard Pares and A. J. P. Taylor (London, 1956), p. 112.
57. Dodington, *Diary*, pp. 333–37.
58. Newcastle to Hardwicke, 12 October 1755, B.M. Add. MS. 32,860, f. 18.

is not so weak a One, as may have been imagined."[59] Furthermore, there were signs of still greater fragmentation in the enemy camp. Egmont approached the First Lord with a proposal for a "pro forma" opposition on the subsidy treaties alone, implying that Lee and others at Leicester House were interested too. Might they, after such a performance, "then be forgiven, & negotiated with?" Newcastle refused the offer, but could not help but be encouraged by the obvious sign of division among his opponents.[60] It was beginning to appear as if Leicester House would not only fail to gain a majority against the subsidies, an unlikely contingency in any case, but that they might not even show sufficient strength to frighten Newcastle—the absolute prerequisite for all their plans.

Pitt, Legge, and George Grenville, all still members of the government, were noticeably absent from the traditional meeting of administration supporters at the Cockpit on the night before the opening of Parliament. Henry Fox, whose promotion to secretary of state had already been arranged, though not announced, took Legge's place as government leader. The following day, the opposition began by a challenge of the address from the throne. In the Commons, the debate over the clause commending the subsidy treaties lasted until five in the morning. The oratorical honors went to the opposition, but the vote to the ministry, 331 to 105.[61] There was no division in the upper house, where Lord Temple had attacked the government almost alone. Pitt, Legge, Grenville, Egmont, and Dodington all spoke against the address, but the last two showed a marked reluctance to push Newcastle too far.[62]

Not even Newcastle was willing to permit latitudinarianism within his government to go this far. On November 20, Pitt,

---

59. Newcastle to Hardwicke, 18 October 1755, B.M. Add. MS. 32,860, f. 89.
60. Newcastle to Hardwicke, 12 October 1755, B.M. Add. MS. 32,860, f. 14.
61. Torrens, *Cabinets*, II, 224.
62. Walpole, *George II*, II, 54.

Grenville, and Legge were all dismissed from office. Bute immediately wrote Grenville:

> I must tell you, my worthy friend, what I should have wished you would have told me on such an occasion; 'tis glorious to suffer in such a cause and with such companions; in times like these, the post of honour is a private situation. I own I from my heart congratulate you.[63]

And Pitt wrote Bute in a similar vein: "Good-night my dear Lord: I believe I shall sleep very quietly and wake as happy as any Minister now in England. Heaven defend and prosper the great cause we have the glory to serve."[64]

There could now be no question of turning back. The opposition continued to harass the administration throughout the rest of the session on the subsidies and the policy of continental warfare which they implied. Since there was no possibility of winning divisions, the debates tended to degenerate into personal abuse, and "the highest Billingsgate rhetoric."[65]

Though Newcastle might be pleased with his majorities, he still had much to worry about. George II was now incensed. He harangued Newcastle on "the extravagent Behaviour of Leicester House. . . . the open Countenance given to Those in the most violent opposition &c." The king even proposed that

> the Two houses should address the King to remove from the P[rince]ss All Persons, who have endeavoured to create Misunderstandings in the Royal Family, by which H[is] M[ajesty] means particularly My L[ord] B[ute].

When Newcastle told the king that he considered this idea impracticable, that "it would be expected that some proof

---

63. Bute to George Grenville, 20 November 1755, *Grenville Papers*, I, 148–49.
64. Pitt to Bute, 20 November [1755], Sedgwick, "Pitt Letters," p. 113.
65. Chesterfield to Solomon Dayrolles, 19 December 1755, in Dobree, *Chesterfield Letters*, V, 2170.

should be made," George II replied that "Impeachments have often been upon *Publick Fame* only."[66] Newcastle and Hardwicke managed to dissuade the king from such rash action, but it was obvious that Augusta's pretence of having no connection with the opposition had failed.

The First Lord was also faced with the problem that would be created by a continuing opposition, which, "considering the King's age, will soon become very formidable."[67] Newcastle had already commented on the fact that Leicester House was particularly attractive to younger men.[68] If the opposition continued, and especially if it were strengthened by new reverses in the war, then the ministry would be faced with the necessity of taking stronger steps to destroy it.

66. Newcastle to Hardwicke, 28 December 1755, B.M. Add. MS. 35,415, ff. 135–37.
67. Hartington to Devonshire, 8 November 1755, in Torrens, *Cabinets*, II, 239.
68. Newcastle to Hardwicke, 12 October 1755, B.M. Add. MS. 32,860, f. 16.

THREE

## LORD BUTE BECOMES GROOM OF THE STOLE

The alliance between Leicester House and the opposition was soon put to its first test. The union of the two parties had been based on limited mutual interest. The tie with the heir apparent gave Pitt and his friends added prestige for their "formed opposition." At the same time, the coalition strengthened Augusta's hand in dealing with George II and his ministers. But the ultimate aims of the two parties were quite different—Pitt seeking power, Augusta security within the royal family—and the strength of their union was thus debatable. In 1756 Prince George's coming of age raised the question of whether their alliance could last if one of the parties seemed to be purchasing its desires at the expense of the other.

The prince's eighteenth birthday was important. It meant that there would be no regency should George II die, and thus decreased the threat of the Duke of Cumberland. It also meant that the prince would now be surrounded by the horde of well paid courtiers suitable to his new station. Two possibilities were represented by this vastly increased establishment. On the one hand, it offered numerous positions which Newcastle could use to reward the faithful.[1] On the other hand, the household could, as Frederick's had, become the nucleus for a new and enlarged opposition, and the Civil List funds could be used to build up a political faction.

[1] Particularly desirable positions because they were not covered by the Place Acts.

George, Prince of Wales, the man for whom this establishment was intended, had thus far received little attention in the turmoil surrounding Leicester House. He was not a normal boy of seventeen. Despite elaborate plans for his education, it had, at best, been spotty. When he was thirteen Princess Augusta characterized her son as "backward."[2] This backwardness was reflected in more than just his formal education. Obstinate and sullen, indolent and moody, George had been excluded from the company of young people because they "were so ill educated and so very vicious, that they frightened" his mother.[3] By the time Bute reappeared at Leicester House, the prince showed, as one psychoanalyst has said, "a striking degree of emotional infantilism."[4] He was unable to concentrate or to apply himself, and he tended to pout and harbor grudges.

Young George soon saw Lord Bute as "his safeguard, his friend, and his comforter."[5] Possibly because Bute represented all the qualities in which the prince was so deficient—handsome, self-assured, well educated—George came to look upon the earl as his "dearest Friend," and "a valuable treasure." Under Bute's guidance he promised to work harder to overcome his "indifference" and "indolence." "I am young and unexperienc'd," he wrote, and "shall exactly follow your advice, without which I shall inevitably sink." "I daily return Heaven thanks, for having met with such a friend as you." The depth of the prince's devotion is difficult to understand unless it is remembered that he was immature, that he had been isolated from society, and that he felt extremely insecure. Within a year of Bute's reintroduction to Leicester House in 1755, the earl was in complete charge of the prince's education,

2. Walpole, *George II*, I, 80; Dodington, *Diary*, p. 187.
3. Waldegrave, *Memoirs*, pp. 8–10; Dodington, *Diary*, p. 152.
4. Manfred S. Guttmacher, *America's Last King* (New York, 1941), p. 26.
5. Shelburne, "Autobiography," p. 53.

and George looked to him for advice on all matters from mode of dress to the nature of the English constitution.[6]

This relationship was not one sided. If the prince adored and idolized Bute, the latter lavished a loyalty on the future king which is reminiscent of the ties between clansman and chief in the Scottish Highlands.[7] There is no evidence to support the frequent allegations that Bute intentionally ingratiated himself with the prince as part of a plot fomented by himself and the princess dowager. The basis for this contention was the alleged illicit relationship between the earl and Augusta. Though this relationship was widely assumed at the time, the evidence is slim, resting primarily on the assertions of the notoriously biased Horace Walpole.[8] The prince's devotion to Bute is more easily and plausibly explained by his supplying the self-assured and confident tutelage which George so desperately needed.[9]

While Bute's influence over the prince was growing, a great deal of attention was being paid to the formation of the heir's household. By late 1755 anxious friends and relatives were already laying plans for advancing their protégés by placing them close to the heir.[10] Newcastle was well aware of this widespread interest. On February 19, 1756, over three months before any proposals were made to Leicester House, Newcastle, Hardwicke, and Lord Waldegrave, the prince's gover-

---

6. The quotations in this paragraph are from the letters of the Prince of Wales to Bute in Sedgwick, *Letters from George III*, and the Bute MSS.

7. E.g. Bute to Gilbert Elliot, 16 August 1756, Minto MSS, National Library of Scotland; Lawrence Henry Gipson, *The British Empire Before the American Revolution* (New York, 1954), VII, 51.

8. For discussions of this problem, and of the unreliability of Walpole on Bute's relationship with Augusta, see Sir Lewis Namier, "George III and Bute," *Avenues of History* (London, n.d.), pp. 118–21; Gerrit P. Judd, *Horace Walpole's Memoirs* (London, 1960), pp. 82–83.

9. For a more thorough examination of this question see Sedgwick, *Letters from George III*, pp. liv–lvi.

10. Chesterfield to Lord Huntingdon, 25 October 1755, Dobree, *Chesterfield Letters*, V, 2164.

nor, held their first formal conference on the subject. The cause of this meeting was a suggestion the prince had made to Waldegrave, that he should at least be allowed to name one member of his household "without any conditions whatsoever." As this obviously meant Lord Bute, whom the king had already thought of impeaching, it was not a prospect which pleased Newcastle. He and his associates proposed to George II that the prince should be removed to the royal palace at Kensington, where he could be surrounded by "proper persons," who would "influence his mind, & remove prejudices." Such an "imprisonment" could then be sweetened by giving the prince a "liberal" establishment of £50,000 a year.[11]

By the time more specific arrangements were made in mid-April, the king had cut the allowance to £40,000, and the primary objective of the plan had become the idea of moving the prince away from Leicester House. Young George and his mother were denied any say in the appointments to be made. The only concession was a promise that the king would "communicate" the establishment to the prince "before it is finally concluded."[12] All of this was formulated by Newcastle and his closest advisers; the ministry as a whole, and Fox in particular, were never included in these discussions.[13]

Newcastle's natural inclination was to postpone unpleasant actions, but when he heard of "a Resolution to propose an Address for settling a provision on the P. of W. in case Parliamt. sits a day after the Birthday" (June 4), the duke must have dreamt of another 1737, when Prince Frederick's supporters had almost carried a motion increasing the prince's allowance in the House of Commons. After a few further inconclusive consultations,[14] the letters informing George and

11. Newcastle, "Memds.," 19 February 1756, B.M. Add. MS. 32,996, f. 359.
12. "Newcastle House," 14 April 1756, B.M. Add. MS. 32,996, ff. 407–8.
13. Dodington, *Diary*, p. 342.
14. J. West to Newcastle, 8 May 1756, B.M. Add. MS. 32,864, f. 499; Chesterfield to Newcastle, 17 May 1756, B.M. Add. MS. 32,865, f. 37.

Augusta of the intended changes were delivered by Lord Waldegrave on May 30.

Effusive replies were returned by the prince and princess, praising His Majesty's "gracious intentions," "Paternal tenderness," and "great goodness." But both letters contained at least a hint of sarcasm. It seemed more than just the flowery expressions of royalty when the Prince of Wales wrote that he lacked "words to express the Sense He had of His Majesty's tenderness towards Him in consulting what is proper for His Rank, Dignity, and Age, and in condiscending to declare the Establishment for His Family shall be communicated to Him, before it is finally concluded."[15] And the princess's letter, as Horace Walpole pointed out, could be read in two different ways.[16] In any case, the prince appeared to have accepted the £40,000 a year, while requesting at the same time to remain with his mother, since "her happiness depends upon their not being seperated." Newcastle and the king were certainly placed in an awkward situation. Could they revoke the offer of an establishment because the prince expressed a laudable desire to remain with his mother? They could scarcely carry off the prince bodily—if only because they remembered the threat of habeas corpus when George II was locked up by his father in 1717. While they were considering the problems raised by the answers, still further difficulties emerged.

The day after the exchange of letters between Kensington and Kew, Andrew Stone told Newcastle that the prince and princess still wanted Bute for "one of the principal Posts in His R.H.'s Family."[17] Newcastle was offered a way of reingratiating himself at Leicester House, of atoning for the events of the previous summer, if he wanted to promote Bute's candidacy against the wishes of the king.

15. Prince of Wales to George II, [30 May 1756], B.M. Add. MS. 32,684, f. 91.
16. Princess of Wales to George II, [30 May 1756], B.M. Add. MS. 32,684, f. 90; Walpole, *George II*, II, 207.
17. Stone to Newcastle, May 31 [1756], B.M. Add. MS. 32,865, ff. 161–62.

Newcastle was now faced with a real dilemma. The advice he had given the king, although it had pleased George II, had resulted in an intensification of the difficulties in the royal family, rather than their solution. As Horace Walpole said, "how little the ministers, who had planned the first step, knew what to advise for the second, was plain."[18] The duke first attempted to continue in the direction already laid down. Waldegrave was sent to Kew to warn the heir that his attitude "would not do," and that he and his mother were on the "Brink of a Precipice." The king had "Absolute Power" over the prince, and was "determined to make Use of His Power" to exclude Bute, whom the king considered too closely connected with Pitt and the opposition to be a suitable companion for the heir apparent. The prince listened quietly, and then disingenuously asked "what the Duke of Newcastle would do?"[19]

The same theme was repeated by Princess Augusta. When Waldegrave approached her, Augusta said that she "had expected more from the Duke of Newcastle, after what She had said to Mr. Stone, That She should make one more Tryal . . . and if She found that made no Impression, She should then trouble the D. of Newcastle no more."[20] The threat was clear, but the duke feared the anger of the king even more than he desired the good will of the heir. As he wrote Hardwicke, "I never saw the King more agitated than he was yesterday."[21]

Newcastle could take some comfort from the fact that George II was still pleased with him for his firm position, but there was not much solace for the duke in the king's other opinions. He had had second thoughts about the £40,000 allowance, and he wanted Prince Edward's establishment to be included in it. This miserliness was troublesome enough, but

18. Walpole, *George II*, II, 208.
19. Newcastle to Hardwicke, 12 June 1756, B.M. Add. MS. 32,865, ff. 279–80; cf. Prince of Wales to Bute, 6 o'clk [9 June 1756], Sedgwick, *Letters from George III*, p. 2.
20. *Ibid.*, f. 282.   21. *Ibid.*, f. 284.

even more disturbing was George II's determination to exclude Lord Bute in spite of Princess Augusta's statement that she and her son requested only one thing, Bute, and "to that they adher'd to the last."[22]

Newcastle sought escape from these worries by turning to his favorite activity, the arranging of appointments, specifically the naming of the new household for the Prince of Wales. Even here there were problems. The Duke of Queensberry withdrew his son from consideration, stating that "common report" indicated that the prince would not be pleased with "the Persons to be put about him," unless the favor he had asked of the king were granted.[23] The prince's statement was actually even stronger; he declared that, if he were not given Bute, he would not recognize any other appointees as "His servants."[24] Many aristocrats, fearful of antagonizing the heir of a seventy-three-year-old monarch, took a stand similar to Queensberry's. Newcastle, after one of his fits of "resigning fever," told Hardwicke that "I don't well see, How a Plan of an Establishment can well be now form'd, Can We in these Circumstances, put in People of Quality, without speaking first to them? & in My Conscience, they will almost *All* refuse."[25]

George II wanted to stop the whole proceeding, but the political implications of this were too much for Newcastle, who soon came up with a plan to evade the principal problem by offering Bute "any proper Mark of His [the King's] Grace and Favor, Except that of an Employment about His Royal Highness, the Prince of Wales."[26] William Murray, as a Scot, was selected to approach the Duke of Argyll with his proposal. Argyll agreed to sound out his nephew, but without much hope of

22. *Ibid.*, ff. 279, 282–84.
23. Queensberry to Newcastle, 22 June 1756, B.M. Add. MS. 32,865, f. 395; "Newcastle House," 23 June 1756, B.M. Add. MS. 32,996, f. 448.
24. Newcastle to Hardwicke, 29 June 1756, B.M. Add. MS. 32,865, f. 464.
25. Newcastle to Hardwicke, 27 June 1756, B.M. Add. MS. 32,865, ff. 447–48.
26. Newcastle to Murray, 9 July 1756, B.M. Add. MS. 32,866, f. 103.

success. He told Murray that "He had wished for years to have connected Ld. B. with the Administration to which Ld. B. was Himself extream'ly well disposed; but the being slighted & passed over; had wrought & might still work upon his Passions."[27]

Another approach was tried at the same time. George II sent a message to his grandson, chiding him for his behavior and demanding an explanation.[28] In his reply the prince repeated his request for permission to stay with his mother, and also mentioned, for the first time officially, his "most ardent request" for Bute.[29]

A stalemate had been reached. The Prince of Wales would accept no establishment that did not include the Earl of Bute, and the king refused to consider that possibility. Many of the ministers advocated breaking off the whole negotiation, but Newcastle, frightened by the spectre of an enlarged opposition when Parliament convened in the fall, persuaded them to persist for a while longer.[30]

The Duke of Marlborough had just told Newcastle that, unless the prince got his way, "there would be the most violent, & determined Opposition, and that levelled singly against" the First Lord.[31] Marlborough added that the government might well be weakened by divisions among the ministers. This idea was reinforced by murmurings from Fox, irritated by his exclusion from the policy discussions of the summer, and also disturbed by the prospect of his difficulties as the leader in the House of Commons if the opposition should renew in the fall.[32] It was clear that the opposition would be

27. Murray to Newcastle, 10 July 1756, B.M. Add. MS. 32,866, f. 111–12.
28. Newcastle to Murray, 9 July 1756, B.M. Add. MS, 32,866, f. 105.
29. Prince of Wales to George II, 12 July 1756, B.M. Add. MS. 32,684, ff. 92–93.
30. Walpole, *George II*, II, 222–23.
31. Newcastle to Hardwicke, 12 July 1756, B.M. Add. MS. 32,866, ff. 141–42.
32. J. West to Newcastle, 24 July 1756, B.M. Add. MS. 32,866, ff. 268–69; Newcastle to Hardwicke, 26 July 1756, B.M. Add. MS. 32,866, ff. 275–76.

strengthened, not only by the apparent ill treatment of the Prince of Wales, but even more by the poor progress of the war and the fall of Minorca.[33] On top of all this, the only other capable spokesman for the ministry in the Commons, Murray, was about to become chief justice and demanded a peerage. How, Fox asked, could he be expected to manage the house under these circumstances?

The leading figures at Leicester House were no happier than Newcastle and the king at the way things were developing. When Augusta had Stone tell Newcastle of her son's desire for Lord Bute, she had obviously expected the duke to leap at the chance of doing her a favor. Newcastle's failure to seize this opportunity greatly complicated the situation by closing the easiest route to compromise, and when George II brought the whole matter into the open by publicly mentioning Bute, it was all too much for the tiny court.

At the end of June, Bute suggested that the simplest solution might be for him to leave Leicester House. Prince George was horrified:

> It is very true that the Ministers have done everything they can to provoke me, that they have call'd me a harmless boy, and have not even deign'd to give me an answer when I so earnestly wish to see my Friend about me . . . .
>
> I know few things I ought to be more thankfull for to the Great Power above, than for its having pleas'd Him to send you to help and advise me in these difficult times.
>
> I do hope you will from this instant banish all thoughts of leaving me . . .[34]

---

33. Leicester House was jubilant when London and other cities sent critical addresses to the ministry: [Lord Talbot to Bute, 18 August 1756], Bute MSS; Bute to Gilbert Elliot, 16 August 1756, Minto MSS, National Library of Scotland.

34. Prince of Wales to Bute, 31 (sic) June 1756, Sedgwick, *Letters from George III*, pp. 2–4.

And Princess Augusta, when she forwarded her son's letter to Bute, said that she could not "express the joy" she felt that Bute had "gaind the confidence and friendship" of her son. "Ld. Bute," she concluded, "forbids his best friend to speak what she feels, but he must allow her to be grateful."[35]

Bute clearly had the support of the prince and princess. In mid-August he wrote a letter to Gilbert Elliot which shows that he was equally committed to them. He told Elliot that the affair of the prince's establishment was still unchanged, that Newcastle could find "no man rash enough" to accept office against the prince's will. Bute reported himself in "good spirits" and encouraged by the "flame now rising" throughout England against the ministry. Despite the fact that "I have experienc'd the Malice of a people that ought to love me," the earl wrote, it did not matter, for young George's devotion and friendship had confirmed Bute in his task, and made him sure of "future Triumphs." Most importantly,

> My Young friend, My hopes, the only Hopes the Spes ultima of this poor countrey, grows every day more firm, More steady; May his future Subjects, be as fond of Liberty as he is; May they have as Strong an aversion to Vice, Corruption & Arbitrary Power, & they will be a happy people; He a happy [prince]. but this is too much to expect, wee have read of Generous nations who asserting their liberty, have forced their Monarchs to be satisfied with a Scanty power; but in what history shall wee find a prostituted people oblidg'd to accept of Freedom, from a Young prince; who preferrs a private life, even to a diadem; unless tis attended with a cap of maintenance, a scepter of Liberty; who is determin'd to rule in the hearts of men, not over the bodys of slaves; this sounds Roman-

---

35. Princess of Wales to Bute, [1 July 1756], Sedgwick, *Letters from George III*, p. 4.

tick yet if this poor nation remains till the time of tryal comes: the experiment will for the first be try'd . . .[36]

These ideas are the stock expressions of eighteenth century opposition, but Bute and the prince firmly believed them. The sense of mission and duty implicit in these beliefs helps explain why there was such concern at Leicester House about what would normally seem a routine appointment. Lord Bute, to Prince George, represented his one hope for forcing "freedom" on his oppressed people.

It could not be expected that their allies would feel as deeply about the appointment of Bute as the princess and her son did. Pitt and his associates suspected that the abandonment of opposition might be the price Augusta would be forced to pay to secure Bute,[37] and the conduct of the princess and her favorite supported this view. During the late summer Leicester House refrained from any attacks on the ministry. Waldegrave told Newcastle in September that "for this last Month, neither the Princess, nor Lord Bute, have talked against Measures, and the Administration, as They used to."[38] Both Pitt and Lee appeared to be out of favor with the princess dowager,[39] and the political world buzzed with rumors when Pitt was received with "coolness" at Leicester House.[40] This friction among their opponents, combined with the unquestioned ascendancy of Bute at the young court,[41] played a large part in influencing Newcastle and his associates to surrender to

36. Bute to Gilbert Elliot, 16 August 1756, Minto MSS, National Library of Scotland.
37. Newcastle to Hardwicke, 2 September 1756, B.M. Add. MS. 35,416, f. 4.
38. Newcastle, "Memorandum with Lord Waldegrave," 16 September 1756, B.M. Add. MS. 32,867, f. 336.
39. Dr. Samuel Squire to Newcastle, [22 August 1756], B.M. Add. MS. 32,867, f. 84; Rigby to the Duke of Bedford, 25 September 1756, *Bedford Correspondence*, II, 199.
40. Newcastle to Hardwicke, 2 September 1756, B.M. Add. MS. 32,867, ff. 179, 181.
41. Squire to Newcastle, [26 August 1756], B.M. Add. MS. 32,867, f. 84.

the demand for Bute in hopes of splitting the forces arrayed against them.

When the Duke of Argyll reported in late August that his mission to Bute had been a total failure, it became apparent that Newcastle would have to give in. Bute had told his uncle that if he were appointed Groom of the Stole, he was sure he could encourage the prince's natural affection for the king, but he insisted that he could accept no other place.[42] Newcastle still toyed with other expedients, like appointing Egmont chancellor of the Exchequer, as the princess's "particular Friend,"[43] or increasing the prince's allowance to £45,000, but the only real alternative would be a promise to create seven or eight peers, including Egmont and Lee, at the end of the parliamentary session, and it was highly unlikely that the king would ever agree to that.[44]

It was, in fact, too late for anything but the appointment of Bute, and, as Newcastle himself suggested, it was probably too late for even that concession to have the desired effect of tying Leicester House to the ministry.[45] Perhaps, if Augusta were really satisfied with the naming of Bute, it would be possible to bring Pitt into the administration as well, and then all problems would be solved.[46] But when Newcastle broached the subject to the king on September 3, His Majesty replied that he still wanted to avoid both Bute and Pitt.[47]

By the middle of September, George II had surrendered.[48] Just how he was brought around is not known, but it seems

42. Murray to Newcastle, 25 August 1756, B.M. Add. MS. 32,867, ff. 46–47.
43. Squire to Newcastle, [26 August 1756], B.M. Add. MS. 32,867, f. 84; see also Lady Yarmouth's statement: Newcastle to Hardwicke, 2 September 1756, B.M. Add. MS. 35,416, f. 3.
44. Newcastle to Hardwicke, 28 August 1756, B.M. Add. MS. 32,867, f. 113.
45. *Ibid.*, f. 119.
46. Hardwicke to Newcastle, 29 August 1756, B.M. Add. MS. 32,867, f. 114.
47. Newcastle to Hardwicke, 3 September 1756, B.M. Add. MS. 32,867, f. 185.
48. Newcastle, "Memds. for the King," 12 September 1756, B.M. Add. MS. 32,867, f. 290; Newcastle to Hardwicke, 18 September 1756, B.M. Add. MS. 32,867, f. 325.

that Newcastle, once convinced that Bute's appointment was essential, found a scapegoat in Fox, who had been urging the advancement of both Pitt and Bute throughout the summer.[49] In this way Newcastle hoped both to avoid the king's wrath for a distasteful action and to bar Fox from taking the credit in the eyes of the prince and princess.

Newcastle now faced the problem of wringing the greatest possible return out of the concession. Fear of a strong opposition had caused Bute's appointment, but was there any way to be sure that this act would really decrease the political activities of Leicester House? Assurances of good behavior from the prince and princess would help, but the wording was a ticklish problem. If too specific pledges were demanded it would seem insulting; if too general, they might be open to varying interpretations. It took almost three weeks for Newcastle and Hardwicke to work out a satisfactory formula and even then it was only at the last minute that they managed to delete from the king's letter a clause demanding that the prince promise to support the ministry.[50]

Lord Waldegrave carried the king's messages to the prince and princess on October 4. Young George, "in a Rapture of Joy," "shew'd all the Satisfaction, and Gratitude, that was possible."[51] Waldegrave then returned to Kensington with letters from the princess dowager and the Prince of Wales, letters "as full of Duty, & Gratitude as possible, & with which His Majesty is very much pleased."[52] Although both replies overflowed with noble sentiments, they contained no specific promises, only general professions of loyalty to the king and to the unity of

49. Memorandum, 3 August 1756, B.M. Add. MS. 32,997, f. 16; Fox to Devonshire, 7 September 1756, Torrens, *Cabinets*, II, 306.
50. Hardwicke to Newcastle, 19 September 1756, B.M. Add. MS. 32,867, f. 340; Hugh Valence Jones to Hardwicke, 2 October 1756, B.M. Add. MS. 35,416, ff. 53–55, 59.
51. Newcastle to Hardwicke, 10 October 1756, B.M. Add. MS. 32,868, f. 167; Newcastle to Fox, 5 October 1756, B.M. Add. MS. 32,868, f. 84.
52. Newcastle to Hardwicke, 5 October 1756, B.M. Add. MS. 35,416, f. 65.

the royal family.⁵³ Hardwicke, as soon as he received the texts, pointed out that "these assurances may be understood as being restrain'd to the *Person of the King*" and not to his ministry. Hardwicke urged Newcastle to take the initiative and approach Pitt, for "unless something of this nature is done, I think this Transaction will not have its full effect." This, he said, must be done at once, before the opposition could recover from the "suddenness of this Turn," and make new arrangements with Leicester House.⁵⁴

It was far too late for the ministers to make any profit from the naming of Bute. Less than a week after the king's messages were delivered, it was widely known that Augusta and Prince George felt they owed nothing to Newcastle and his henchmen.⁵⁵ And George II destroyed any lasting benefit he might have gained from the affair when he petulantly refused to speak to Bute when the earl appeared at Court to receive the appointment of Groom of the Stole. Instead, the sovereign had the Duke of Grafton give the gold key of the office to Bute.⁵⁶ Little wonder that Bute, when he was wished joy of his new place by Grafton, replied that he felt none so long as Newcastle was in office.⁵⁷

Newcastle, by his procrastination and indecision, had lost whatever opportunity he had to secure the support of Leicester House. Had George II been advised earlier that it was absolutely necessary to accept Bute, and had the king done so with good grace, it might have been possible to convince Leicester House of the advantages of cooperating with the

---

53. For the full text of the king's messages, see B.M. Add. MS. 32,868, ff. 86, 88; for the prince and princess's replies, B.M. Add. MS. 32,684, ff. 95–96.

54. Newcastle to Hardwicke, 7 October 1756, B.M. Add. MS. 32,868, ff. 120–21.

55. Newcastle to Hardwicke, 10 October 1756, B.M. Add. MS. 32,868, f. 163; Waldegrave, *Memoirs*, p. 78.

56. Waldegrave, *Memoirs*, p. 79; Walpole, *George II*, II, 259; Fox to Lord Digby, 28 October 1756, HMC, *8th Report*, Pt. 1, 222.

57. Walpole, *George II*, II, 259.

ministry. But this was certainly not the lesson the prince and princess learned in the end. By waiting until the approach of a stormy parliamentary session forced his hand, Newcastle proved to Augusta and Bute, not that he was their friend, but that their best hope for receiving what they wanted lay in close cooperation with the opposition. Pitt and his supporters had played no direct role in the dealings of the summer,[58] but if Augusta and her son had not been associated with the opposition, Newcastle need not have worried about their influence in Parliament, and the king would not have been forced to give in. As a result of their mismanagement of the whole affair, Newcastle and George II not only saw the chief position at Leicester House occupied by a nominee fully aware of their attempts to block his appointment, but they also sacrificed any benefit they might have gained from this concession. For Newcastle, particularly, the long season of negotiation and bargaining was to no avail—within a month he was out of office.

58. Pitt has been incorrectly credited with aiding Bute's candidacy on the basis of a letter from Bute to Pitt, mistakenly dated 3 June 1756 in *Chatham Correspondence*, I, 156–58: Williams, *Pitt*, I, 282; Brian Tunstall, *William Pitt, Earl of Chatham* (London, 1938), p. 159; O. A. Sherrard, *Lord Chatham: Pitt and the Seven Years' War* (London, 1956), p. 125. This letter should be dated 6 July 1758: Sedgwick, "Pitt Letters," p. 156.

FOUR

## THE FORMATION OF THE PITT-NEWCASTLE MINISTRY

Lord Bute's position at Leicester House was now assured, and for the next four years his ascendancy over the Prince and Princess of Wales remained unquestioned. His former competitors, men like Cresset and Egmont who had played leading roles in the princess's family before the rise of Bute, quickly disappeared from the scene.[1] Even Sir George Lee, who in 1755 had considered himself *the* adviser to the princess dowager, found that Bute had so thoroughly displaced him that he resigned in disgust in June, 1757.[2] The new appointees to Prince George's household offered the earl no challenge. Though many of them came into their positions with hopes of gaining the confidence of the heir,[3] they all failed. The prince made it plain that he desired "never to see them except upon his court days,"[4] and the more perceptive of the newcomers soon abandoned their attempt to cultivate the prince and began trying to ingratiate themselves with Bute instead.[5]

While the dominance of Bute at Leicester House was evi-

1. James Cresset to Newcastle, 7 October 1756, B.M. Add. MS. 32,868, ff. 131–32.
2. Horace Walpole to Sir Horace Mann, 20 June 1757, W. S. Lewis, *et al.*, eds., *Yale Edition of Horace Walpole's Correspondence* (New Haven, 1937–), XXI, 104; Glover, *Memoirs*, p. 72.
3. Chesterfield to Huntingdon, 30 October 1756, 6 November 1756, Dobree, *Chesterfield Letters*, V, 2205–6, 2207.
4. Fox to Lord Digby, 28 October 1756, HMC, *8th Report*, Pt. I, 222.
5. Lord Pembroke to Bute, 9 February 1757, Bute MSS; Lord Bathurst to Bute, [5 October 1756], Bute MSS; see Chesterfield's advice to Lord Huntingdon, 18 November 1756, Dobree, *Chesterfield Letters*, V, 2206.

dent, it was not at all clear that the connection between the prince's court and the opposition had weathered the summer. Pitt, in particular, was concerned about the implications of a *detente* between the two branches of the royal family. The outward signs of friendship continued. Pitt congratulated Bute on his appointment,[6] and when Bute sent glowing compliments on the birth of Pitt's first son,[7] Pitt returned in kind: "Lady Hester is safely deliver'd of a Boy; who I think will live one day to be an Englishman, and to bless, together with millions yet unborn, the happy influence of the princely virtues Ld Bute cultivates so successfully."[8] These warm phrases could not, however, conceal Pitt's suspicion over Bute's appointment. When, in October, the ministry appeared on the brink of collapse, Pitt resolved to seek office without consulting Leicester House.

The Newcastle administration was reeling from a series of major setbacks. Admiral Byng's defeat at Minorca and the fall of Oswego were bad enough, but when Frederick the Great, England's new ally, invaded Saxony, Newcastle's nightmare had come true—an unprepared Britain was involved in a full scale continental war. On top of these disasters, the duke's political empire was rapidly crumbling. Murray, despite Newcastle's feverish attempts to bribe him into remaining in the House of Commons, had become chief justice, thus removing one of the few able government spokesmen from the Commons. The final blow came on October 15, when Fox, angered by his exclusion from key policy and patronage decisions, announced his intention of resigning.

Even Newcastle realized that Pitt was now essential; only the Great Commoner could revive public confidence in the

---

6. Pitt to Bute, 7 October 1756, Bute MSS, Sedgwick, "Pitt Letters," pp. 114–15.
7. Bute to Pitt, Sunday [10 October 1756], PRO 30/8/24, f. 291.
8. Pitt to Bute, [10 October 1756], Bute MSS, Sedgwick, "Pitt Letters," p. 115.

government. When Lord Hardwicke asked Pitt to a meeting, the latter agreed, but expressly "resolved to go to this conference without previous participation with Lord B[ute]."[9] The negotiation was a complete failure. Pitt demanded a total change in the principal officeholders, and this the king refused even to consider. Pitt, never a very practical politician, began to sense what many observers had already pointed out: that he did not have sufficient influence to gain power without the support of Leicester House. A few days later Henry Fox reported that "this transaction has made Pitt and Ld. Bute friends again."[10] Fox's own activities had also drawn them together. Since his resignation, the late secretary had been trying desperately to form a new government, headed by himself.[11] When he made no progress with either Legge or Pitt, Fox tried a direct approach to Bute.[12] Fox, to Leicester House, meant Cumberland, and their fear of the duke, who was once again the undoubted favorite at St. James's, drove Princess Augusta and Bute back to Pitt. By early November Gilbert Elliot was able to write his wife that "there is the greatest harmony in the World" between Bute and Pitt.[13]

Without Fox and Murray in the Commons and with Pitt absolutely refusing to serve in the cabinet with Newcastle, the duke felt that his position was hopeless. Accordingly, on October 26, Newcastle and Hardwicke told the king they could not continue, and that the only solution was to bring in Pitt. George II hated this idea, and he tried every alternative before finally accepting Pitt.

Bute did not take an active part in the negotiations for es-

9. Pitt to George Grenville, 17 October 1756, *Grenville Papers*, I, 178.
10. Henry Fox to Lord Digby, 25 October 1756, HMC, *8th Report*, I, 221.
11. Hardwicke to Sir Joseph Yorke, 31 October 1756, B.M. Add. MS. 35,357, f. 69.
12. Walpole, *George II*, II, 262, 265; Fox to Bute, 29 October 1756, B.M. Add. MS. 5726, D., f. 46.
13. Elliot to Mrs. Murray, 4 November 1756, Elliot, *Border Elliots*, p. 352.

tablishing the new ministry, but he did make it absolutely clear that Leicester House was resolved "to approve and support to the utmost" whatever Pitt should decide. When some of the participants did not like their split of the spoils, "the Prince of Wales's name was used" by Bute, and they fell into line.[14] It was this unqualified support from the junior branch of the royal family which, as much as Pitt's oratory or popular appeal, brought him at last into power.[15]

The ministry formed in November, 1756, was not, and in fact could not be, a complete change. The Duke of Devonshire, a renowned Whig, became first lord of the Treasury. Lord Holdernesse, at George II's insistence, stayed on as secretary of state and Lord Granville remained president of the Council. None of the major positions at court were filled by the opposition, but Pitt entered the cabinet as the second secretary of state, his brother-in-law Lord Temple became first lord of the Admiralty, and H. B. Legge returned to the Exchequer. Gilbert Elliot, the Grenvilles, and others were provided for in lesser places. Virtually all of the leading members of the opposition came into office, but they were too few to fill all the major places. Large numbers of Newcastle and Fox protégés remained in office, eagerly awaiting the failure of the Pitt experiment.

None of the politicians of the day understood how Pitt could hope to stay in office without the support of either Newcastle or Fox, but the new secretary was determined to try. At forty-nine Pitt had at last achieved a position where he could formulate policy and, as he told the Duke of Devonshire, "I know that I can save this country and no one else can."[16] He had the support of Leicester House and his own little band,

14. Lord Temple to Pitt, [11 November 1756], *Chatham Correspondence*, I, 192–93.
15. Horace Walpole to Sir Horace Mann, 4 November 1756, *Yale Horace Walpole*, XXI, 12–13.
16. Tunstall, *Pitt*, pp. 165–66.

and he was shortly assured of the backing of the Tories.[17] But this was not enough. Newcastle's majority remained loyal to its master, confident that he would soon return to power. And George II still detested Pitt and Temple. He had accepted them because he had no alternative, and it was only Pitt's immense popularity "out of doors" that kept the king from dismissing him. If that popularity should ever weaken, the feeble ministry was obviously lost.

No one was more interested in preserving Pitt than Bute. He and the princess had achieved the height of their ambitions: the leading ministers were their "friends," Cumberland's friends were excluded from the administration, and as an added bonus Newcastle was out as well. This was a happy change from the situation of a few months earlier, when the prince and princess were reduced to begging for Bute's appointment.

Though Bute still refrained from taking any direct political role, he gave all possible support to the ministry. Even when Pitt reversed the traditional opposition policy and requested £200,000 for Hanoverian defense, Bute sent his "sincerest congratulations," and assured Pitt that the Prince of Wales supported the move.[18] The new ministers, in turn, made every attempt to convince Leicester House of their good will. A flood of letters and conferences kept Bute informed of every governmental action and of all military and foreign news.[19] Any request from the earl was immediately granted.[20] And Pitt pledged his allegiance in unmistakable terms:

> The whole devotion of [my heart] is offer'd at . . . . [Leicester House], where your friendship alone cou'd have

17. Fox to Sir Charles Hanbury Williams, 28 December 1756, B.M. Stowe MS. 263, ff. 12–13; Glover, *Memoirs*, p. 64; Walpole, *George II*, II, 316.
18. Bute to Pitt, Saturday [19 February 1757], *Chatham Correspondence*, I, 223–24 (where it is misdated March 2).
19. Bute MSS; see esp. the letters from Gilbert Elliot, William Pitt, Lord Temple and Sir Harry Erskine.
20. E.g. Temple to Bute, 12 March 1757, Bute MSS.

made it appear an undespicable oblation. The most gracious acceptance of my ardent vows for their glory and happiness shall be my perpetual support under every difficulty.[21]

Bute also played an independent role in support of the ministry. When Pitt resolved to raise Highland regiments for service in America, Bute aided in planning the force and selecting the officers.[22] Certain Scottish members of Parliament began to look to Bute for instructions,[23] and one important English convert to the ministry, Lord George Sackville, son of the Duke of Dorset, made it clear that he "chuses that he shou'd be considered as your [Bute's] friend, more than as connected with any other individual of that body of friends."[24] Bute was, in fact, becoming the leader of his own faction whose members looked to the earl for direction in all their political activities.[25] For the time being, all of his influence was used to support Pitt, but if the time ever came when a more independent approach was needed, Bute would be in a strong position to carry it through.

Bute's eager support was not enough, of course, to preserve Pitt in office. The king "became every day more averse to his new ministers,"[26] and Fox and Newcastle bided their time, waiting for the proper opening to bring down the administration. As long as the popularity of the ministry remained high, however, its enemies did not dare to open attack. They did not have to wait long, for the unfortunate Admiral Byng soon supplied them their opportunity.

Byng had been convicted and condemned to death on Janu-

21. Pitt to Bute, February 19 [1757], Bute MSS, Sedgwick, "Pitt Letters," pp. 119–20.
22. S. Fraser to Bute, 3 March 1757, Lord Eglinton to Bute, 23 January 1757, Bute MSS.
23. J. Rose Mackye to Bute, 9 April 1757, 17 April 1757, Bute MSS.
24. Sir Harry Erskine to Bute, Thursday [January 1757], Bute MSS.
25. See Lord Eglinton to Bute, 25 January 1757, Bute MSS.
26. Waldegrave, *Memoirs*, pp. 93–94.

ary 27, 1757, but his judges added a strong plea for mercy. As first lord of the Admiralty, Lord Temple made it clear that he and Pitt favored a royal pardon. It is impossible to determine whether their attitude was motivated by a merciful feeling toward Byng, or by political expediency. Lord Chesterfield expressed the latter view well, if a bit crudely: "the late Admiralty want to shoot him, to excuse themselves; and the present Admiralty want to save him, in order to lay the blame upon their predecessors."[27] The public, however, did not understand the subtleties of the situation; mobs stormed through London chanting, "Hang Byng or take care of your King."

The popularity of the ministers thus began to slip as soon as it was known that they were trying to save the Admiral, and their support of Byng also pushed George II's patience to the breaking point. Early in March, 1757, Sir Harry Erskine glumly reported to Bute that "Our friends I understand are infinitely worse in the Closet than they were some weeks ago."[28] The king's determination was unshaken by the pleas of Pitt and Temple: Byng was executed on March 14, 1757.

It was at this point—with Pitt's popularity badly diminished and the king infuriated by his ministers—that the Duke of Cumberland was proposed to command an "army of observation" which was to be sent to protect the Prussian flank and keep the French out of Hanover. But Cumberland refused to accept the command under a ministry containing numerous adherents of Leicester House.[29] Lord Temple was accordingly dismissed on April 4. Pitt was expected to resign as a result of the affront to his brother-in-law; when he refused to do so, he too was dismissed on April 6, the day before Cumberland

27. Chesterfield to Solomon Dayrolles, 28 February 1757, Dobree, *Chesterfield Letters*, V, 2220.
28. Erskine to Bute, 7 March [1757], Bute MSS.
29. Joseph Yorke to Hardwicke, 22 April 1757, Yorke, *Hardwicke*, II, 395.

left for Germany. Legge, the Grenvilles, and the others who had come in under the protection of Leicester House in November all resigned.

Though the ministry had been in danger for some time, the fact that it was brought down by the Duke of Cumberland seemed to confirm all of the princess's fears. And when the king asked Fox to form a new administration, the Leicester House leaders hurriedly turned to the only alternative, the Duke of Newcastle. Through intermediaries, they let the duke know that "this was the Time" for a combination of Leicester House, Pitt and Newcastle.[30] Legge lost no time in making contact; the day after he resigned the Exchequer seals, he told Lord Anson that he would like to see Newcastle.[31] Newcastle, thinking that Leicester House was "so much frighten'd" by the prospect of a new ministry headed by Fox, that they would accept almost any terms for his assistance,[32] arranged a secret meeting with Legge at Lord Dupplin's house, "where there is a Back Door to the Park."[33] Nothing material resulted from this meeting, but it did weaken the hand of the Leicester House faction, which had been holding aloof from the duke in the hope of improving its bargaining position. Though pledged to silence, Newcastle immediately broadcast the details of the conversation, and Legge found himself on bad terms with Pitt and Bute.[34]

Bute was only a little slower than Legge in making his advances to Newcastle, but he was much more cautious than the ex-chancellor. Every move that Bute made in the complicated negotiations of the next three months was closely coordinated with Pitt, starting with a meeting between Bute and Pitt on

30. Newcastle to Hardwicke, 8 April 1757, B.M. Add. MS. 32,870, f. 387.
31. Hardwicke to Newcastle, 9 April 1757, B.M. Add. MS. 32,870, f. 397.
32. Newcastle to Mansfield, 13 April 1757, B.M. Add. MS. 32,870, ff. 411–12.
33. Newcastle to Hardwicke, 15 April 1757, B.M. Add. MS. 32,870, f. 419.
34. Glover, *Memoirs*, p. 95.

the very night of the latter's dismissal.[35] By April 19 enough progress had been made through indirect channels that Newcastle noted in his memoranda that "Ld. B. desires Connection," though the duke was overly optimistic when he stated that "Leicester House will do, as shall be desired."[36] The view from Leicester House was somewhat different. Sir Harry Erskine, a Scot who was rapidly becoming one of Bute's closest friends, told Bute four days later, that Newcastle "intends to throw himself entirely on Leicester House, he is determin'd to make you his Friend; don't laugh my Lord; he is to be your bosom friend."[37] By this time the area of agreement was small; both sides saw the necessity of combining, and Leicester House had reluctantly accepted the idea that Newcastle must be first lord of the Treasury.[38] There was a long way yet to go.

A meeting between the two principals was the next step, but Bute insisted that before it could occur Newcastle would have to agree to a number of specific points, points which give an interesting insight into the objectives of Leicester House:

> That the Duke of Newcastle should send by my Lord B. a Compliment to the Prince of W. upon His Royal Hss Displeasure with Him, at what past last Summer.
> That the D. of N. should have an Immediate Interview with Ld. B. for that purpose.
> That the D. of N. should settle a constant Correspondence, & Comm[unication] with Ld. B.
> That He should acquaint Him, with what shall pass with regard to Public Affairs, for the Information of ye P. of W.
> That the D. of N. shall assure Ld. B. of His Friendship,

---

35. Pitt to Bute, 4 o'clock Wednesday [6 April 1757], Bute MSS, Sedgwick, "Pitt Letters," pp. 120–21.
36. Claremont, 19 April 1757, B.M. Add. MS. 32,997, f. 135.
37. Sir Harry Erskine to Bute, 23 April 1757, Bute MSS.
38. *Ibid.*

& Support for the Continuance of His Confidence with the P. of W.

That the P. of W. shall in return have a Confidence, & Friendship for the D. of N.[39]

That Newcastle's supposed treachery in the affair of the prince's household still rankled is obvious. Two other aspects of this list are of particular interest. One is the insistence that the prince be informed of all that happened "with regard to Public Affairs," a desire which reflected the consistent exclusion of the heir from any governmental functions under the Hanoverians. Leicester House demanded that any minister who wanted to be considered their "friend" must supply detailed intelligence reports. The second point is the lack of any mention of Bute's political allies. It would seem that Bute and the princess were more interested in bringing Newcastle into their orbit, and thus adding to their security, than in bringing about a real partnership between the duke and Pitt, which might lessen the role of the junior court.

Newcastle and Bute met on May 3, at Lord George Sackville's.[40] No record exists of what passed in this "first Conversation of a quite new Acquaintance,"[41] but enough progress was made to justify another meeting three days later.[42] Newcastle was pleased to think that he was now on friendly terms with the Prince of Wales, but he was discouraged by the terms which Bute and Pitt insisted upon for a ministerial settlement.[43] Torn by conflicting advice—Devonshire urging him to form a ministry excluding Leicester House, Chesterfield

---

39. Claremont, 26 April 1757, B.M. Add. MS. 32,997, f. 138.
40. For the evidence supporting this date, see McKelvey, "Bute and George III," p. 123, n. 62.
41. Armagh to Bute, [3 May 1757], Bute MSS; for what Newcastle intended to say see "Paper of Heads," B.M. Add. MS. 32,997, ff. 140–43.
42. Armagh to Bute, Friday past three o'clock [6 May 1757], Wednesday night 4 May [1757], Bute MSS.
43. Newcastle to Chesterfield, 7 May 1757, B.M. Add. MS. 32,871, f. 39.

telling him that no stable ministry could be formed without them—Newcastle procrastinated, and the negotiations degenerated into quibbling.[44]

Despite numerous conversations no progress was made during the remainder of May. Pitt insisted on the dropping of Lord Winchelsea as first lord of the Admiralty, which the king refused, on appointing George Grenville as chancellor of the Exchequer, which Newcastle wouldn't stand, and on the complete exclusion of Fox, to whom George II had promised the Paymastership. Bute, Erskine, Hardwicke and the Archbishop of Armagh all tried to bring the parties together, but their attempts floundered on the obstinacy of Pitt and the equal stubbornness of George II, who preferred to explore every alternative before accepting Pitt. It was not until June 4 that a break occurred. Pitt, frightened by Newcastle's attempt to form a new ministry of his own, dropped his demand that George Grenville be named chancellor of the Exchequer.[45] Newcastle gleefully rose to the bait, but it soon became apparent that the removal of one obstacle—the Chancellorship— did not automatically insure success, for George II persisted in his demand that Fox be named paymaster and that Winchelsea be retained at the Admiralty, while Pitt remained adamantly opposed to both.[46] The angry king was on the verge of appointing a new government, headed by Fox and excluding both Pitt and Newcastle, when Murray, now Lord Mansfield, dissuaded him. On June 11, George II reluctantly gave in; all that he now insisted on was Fox's appointment as paymaster.[47]

44. Stone to Newcastle, 7 May 1757, Chesterfield to Newcastle, Saturday noon [7 May 1757], B.M. Add. MS. 32,871, ff. 36, 45.
45. Chesterfield to Newcastle, June 3 [1757], B.M. Add. MS. 32,871, f. 199; Newcastle to Hardwicke, [4 June 1757], B.M. Add. MS. 32,871, f. 216.
46. George II to Newcastle, 4 June 1757, B.M. Add. MS. 35,416, f. 228; Gilbert Elliot to Lord Minto, 4 June 1757, Minto MSS, National Library of Scotland.
47. Waldegrave, *Memoirs*, p. 129; Newcastle to Bute, 11 June 1757, Bute MSS.

Serious obstacles still remained. The king soon raised his demands to include naming the secretary of war.[48] Pitt gave in and accepted Lord Barrington instead of Lord George Sackville.[49] H. B. Legge, now designed to be chancellor of the Exchequer, was very unhappy at the prospect of serving under the Duke of Newcastle, who he felt had betrayed him in April.[50] Hardwicke, desperately trying to complete the arrangements under the king's orders for haste, asked Bute to approach Legge; "Use Him Gently and Kindly," the chancellor wrote. "Try to gain Him, which You may do. He is disposed to be gained by You."[51] Bute overcame Legge's suspicion of Pitt and Newcastle, and agreement was assured by June 18. An orgy of congratulations followed. Hardwicke wrote Bute that "I have not fail'd to do as much Justice, as my Tongue is capable of expressing, to Your Lordship's noble & public-spirited Sentiments & Conduct throughout this Transaction; and That in the place [the closet], where it might produce the best Effects, and was extremely well receiv'd."[52] In answer Bute modestly disclaimed any credit for himself, but stressed that "whatever success my poor efforts may have had, that ought in Justice to be imputed, solely, to the excellent dispositions of the Young Prince I am devoted to."[53]

With Pitt as secretary of state, Newcastle at the Treasury, and Legge chancellor of the Exchequer, it was a strong administration. Temple became Lord Privy Seal, where the king would seldom see him. Fox disappeared into the lucrative obscurity of the Pay Office. The difficulties which had plagued all ministries since the death of Henry Pelham seemed finally

48. Hardwicke to Newcastle, Wednesday night 12 o'clock [15 June 1757], B.M. Add. MS. 32,871, f. 311.
49. Newcastle to Lord Darlington, 21 June 1757, B.M. Add. MS. 32,871, f. 365.
50. Legge to Bute, 17 June [1757], Bute MSS.
51. Enclosure in Hardwicke to Bute, 17 June 1757, Bute MSS.
52. Hardwicke to Bute, 18 June 1757, Bute MSS; Newcastle echoed the same theme: Newcastle to Bute, 18 June 1757, Bute MSS.
53. Bute to Hardwicke, 20 June 1757, B.M. Add. MS. 35,423, f. 235.

to be solved. All of the major elements in the eighteenth century political world were represented in the union of Pitt and Newcastle. Newcastle controlled Parliament and had the ear of the king; Pitt enjoyed immense popularity and had the confidence of both Leicester House and the "moneyed interest" of the city of London. If the ministers could get along with one another and with the king, the new administration had excellent prospects.

Nonetheless, Pitt and many of his adherents were displeased with the settlement. The new secretary told Hardwicke that it was "a mutilated, enfeebled, half-formed System,"[54] and, in a letter to Bute on the very day before the new appointees took office, Pitt called Newcastle, his partner, a "wretch."[55] Others in the Leicester House group were even less happy. George Grenville felt cheated because Pitt had obtained him nothing better than the Treasurership of the Navy.[56] The Townshends were still more upset, and George Townshend condemned "the ridiculous & dishonest Arrangement of Men which is now to take place."[57] Lord George Sackville, although he had acquiesced in the change, imagined himself unjustly deprived of the Secretaryship at War.[58] H. B. Legge was not only uncomfortable in his return to the Treasury, he was also convinced of Pitt's animosity and angered by the exclusion of his protégé, Samuel Martin, from office.

Relations between the principals at Leicester House, however, could not have been better. When news of Frederick the Great's defeat at Prague reached London two days after the new government took office, Bute wrote Pitt, "Thank God, I

54. Pitt to Hardwicke, Wednesday, 6 o'clock [22 June 1757], B.M. Add. MS. 35,423, ff. 185–86.
55. Pitt to Bute, Tuesday, 11 o'clock [28 June 1757], Bute MSS, Sedgwick, "Pitt Letters," p. 125.
56. "Mr. Grenville's Narrative," *Grenville Papers*, I, 438–39.
57. Townshend's endorsement on William Pitt to George Townshend, 18 June 1757, HMC, *11th Report*, App., Pt. IV (1887), 393.
58. Sir Harry Erskine to Bute, 18 June 1757, Bute MSS.

see you in office. If even the wreck of this crown can be preserved to our amiable young Prince, 'tis to your efforts, your abilities, my dear Pitt, that he must owe it."[59] Pitt, in turn, felt comforted by "the honours, comforts and security of [Bute's] noble and true friendship," and added that he was "unalterably and totally devoted" to the service of the Prince of Wales.[60] Prince George, for his part, assured Bute that "I will keep most steadily to the part so often talk'd of between us, and will with the greatest affection and tenderness be yours till death separates us."[61]

This harmony between the prince, Bute, and Pitt was now to be put to the test of power. With Pitt securely in office, new strains inevitably appeared. Within a year and a half, the Prince's satisfaction with Pitt had changed to bitter denunciations of the "infamous and ungrateful part" played by the Great Commoner.[62]

59. Bute to Pitt, Friday [1 July 1757], *Chatham Correspondence*, I, 241 (misdated August 5).
60. Pitt to Bute, Tuesday, 11 o'clock [28 June 1757], Bute MSS, Sedgwick, "Pitt Letters," pp. 124–45.
61. Prince of Wales to Bute, Friday 11 [10 June 1757?], Sedgwick, *Letters from George III*, pp. 6–7.
62. Prince of Wales to Bute, 9 o'clock [December 1758], Sedgwick, *Letters from George III*, p. 19.

FIVE

## LEICESTER HOUSE AND THE NEW ADMINISTRATION

By 1757 Leicester House had clearly become one of the most important elements in British politics. At the height of the ministerial crisis in June, the Prussian minister in London had reported to Frederick the Great that "L'age avance du roy" made many politicians, including Newcastle and Holdernesse, reluctant to take office without an understanding with "La jeune cour," lest the death of George II should leave them unemployed.[1]

It was this factor, the inevitable demise of the crown and all its powers, which made the heir and his faction of prime importance in all political calculations. The leading figures at Leicester House lived in eager anticipation of George II's death; their letters are full of references to "that Critical minute," "that severe but noblest trial," "that important day."[2] And Prince George was far from pleased when he wrote Bute in November, 1758, that the king was beginning "to gain strength, and is likely to last till summer."[3]

Certainly the leader of the Leicester House group was now quite conscious of his own potential power. As Bute wrote his

---

1. Report of 10 June 1757, in Albert von Ruville, *William Pitt, Earl of Chatham* (London, 1907), II, 124.
2. Bute to Pitt, Tuesday [28 June 1757], PRO 30/8/24, f. 295 (incorrectly docketed 29 August 1757); Pitt to Bute, [30 August 1757], Bute MSS, Sedgwick, "Pitt Letters," p. 130; Bute to Pitt, 4 June 1757, *Chatham Correspondence*, I, 317.
3. Prince of Wales to Bute, past 12 [November 1758], Sedgwick, *Letters from George III*, p. 17.

brother, James Stuart Mackenzie, "The Late Critical Juncture has undoubtedly Brought me into a Great tho' delicate Situation." Although "the Suspicious Censure of angry men" was raised against him, he despised this "Calumny," for he knew he had acted "a noble disinterested Part." He had furthered no views of his own, he had simply supported the prestige of the prince, and the prince's interests were, to Bute, inseparable from the interests of Great Britain. Despite this selfless conduct, Bute's power was already great, and bound to become greater. Mackenzie should not worry because he had received no position in the new administration:

> Put a Firm Confidence in me & don't Blush to own you do so to any Mortell Breathing if my Prospect is a great one Remember you are My Brother whom I Love, Talk of a future day to those who ask you the Kind Questions you mention few of them but wou'd gladly Exchange their Present Emoluments for to stand My Brother, . . .[4]

For the first months following the establishment of the new government, everything seemed to be going Bute's way. He and Pitt met constantly to discuss official business,[5] to commiserate over the difficulties of dealing with Newcastle, and, particularly on Bute's part, to look forward to brighter days.[6] When Pitt, in a stormy cabinet session, managed to defeat a proposal to send English troops to Germany, he attributed his success to Bute and wrote the earl that it was only the consolation of his friendship which gave him the strength "to carry me thro' the distress of the present conjecture."[7]

The partnership of Bute and Pitt was soon crowned with

---

4. [Bute to Mackenzie, July 1757], Bute MSS (draft).
5. Bute MSS, *ad passim*; Sedgwick, "Pitt Letters," *passim*; PRO 30/8/24, *passim*.
6. Bute to Pitt, [28 June 1757], PRO 30/8/24, f. 295.
7. Pitt to Bute, Friday Evening [5 August 1757], Bute MSS, Sedgwick, "Pitt Letters," p. 128.

the best of news. The Duke of Cumberland, having been sent to Germany in the spring with very broad powers, disgraced himself by signing the Convention of Closterseven, which neutralized Hanover. English public opinion was outraged; the duke was recalled and snubbed by his father. He resigned as commander-in-chief of the English army and, for the time being, withdrew from public affairs. Bute and Pitt immediately pushed Lord Ligonier, an elderly but pliable officer, for commander-in-chief, and Lord George Sackville, a Leicester House adherent, for Ligonier's old post as lieutenant general of the Ordnance—thus hoping to extend the influence of the young court into the highest reaches of the army.[8]

The greatest threat to the security of Leicester House was now removed. Though both Pitt and Bute were highly pleased with Cumberland's disgrace, this event marks an important turning point in their relations. This did not become immediately apparent, but gradually Pitt came to find Newcastle a more submissive companion than Bute and the uses of power more absorbing than the petty concerns of Leicester House. Without Cumberland there remained no real threat to the ministry, and there was far less to hold the Scottish courtier and the English statesman together. The immediate concerns of Leicester House—patronage, court intrigue, family grievances—were of little significance to Pitt, whose consequent lack of cooperation irritated the young court. By the time another year had passed the tie was broken which had helped bring Pitt to power and Bute to the center of national politics.

For the moment, however, everyone but the Duke of Cumberland appeared reconciled. Even George II, angry with his son, made gestures of friendship toward his grandson, and presented the prince with a service of plate.[9] Cumberland was

8. Pitt to Bute, [17 October 1757], Bute MSS, Sedgwick, "Pitt Letters," p. 134.
9. Chesterfield to his Son, Bath, 20 November 1757, Dobree, *Chesterfield Letters*, V, 2264.

gone, "the old Court and the young one are much better together";[10] all problems seemed at last to have been solved.

There were still some minor difficulties. Newcastle, acutely conscious of having antagonized the prince in 1756, was now pathetically eager to please the heir,[11] but he was unable to secure George II's permission for the removal of two minor functionaries in the prince's household so that they could be replaced by Leicester House favorites.[12] Three far more important vacancies were created in late 1757 and early 1758 by the death of two of Prince George's Lords of the Bedchamber and the resignation of another.[13] These offices were highly desirable and were always filled by peers or the eldest sons of peers. Prince Frederick had named his closest political friends as his lords. Furthermore, since the lords did have specific duties about the prince, it was preferable to maintain the full contingent so as to prevent an undue burden from falling on one man. Thus Bute and the prince wanted the vacancies filled quickly. But they wanted them filled according to their choice, not that of the king.

By law, appointments to the prince's establishment remained under the control of the king until the heir turned twenty-one.[14] Bute tried to get Newcastle to gain George II's permission for the prince to name whomever he pleased, but the duke fussed and procrastinated.[15] So long as there was a single vacancy this delay was not serious. But when there were two, and then three, pressures built up rapidly. A number of lords had requested Bute's help in being appointed,[16] and the

10. *Ibid.*
11. Newcastle to Bute, 1 July 1757, Bute MSS.
12. Newcastle to Armagh, 20 August 1757, B.M. Add. MS. 32,873, f. 187.
13. Lord Digby d. 26 November 1757, Lord Sussex d. 8 January 1758, the Duke of Grafton apparently resigned late in May, 1758.
14. Hardwicke to Newcastle, 23 November 1759, B.M. Add. MS. 32,899, f. 61.
15. Pitt to Bute, Monday [12 December 1757], Bute MSS, Sedgwick, "Pitt Letters," p. 139; Newcastle, "Memds. for the King," 21 December 1757, B.M. Add. MS. 32,876, f. 365.
16. E.g. Lord Lauderdale to Bute, 3 December 1757, Lord Carnarvon to

danger of antagonizing them, or of their applying directly to George II, which was precisely what Bute did not want,[17] increased considerably as winter passed into spring and no action was taken.

The negotiations were greatly complicated by the Leicester House leader's insistence on complete secrecy. Bute argued that for the prince even to reveal the names of the lords he wanted to appoint would sink the heir to the level of "a Poor Petitioner."[18] Leicester House saw the prince's right "to have the free Choice of his Servants" as a moral issue, and Bute would not even permit Newcastle to know the identity of the intended lords so that he could whisper them to Lady Yarmouth, who could then obtain the king's approval.[19]

Bute's demand, in effect for the prince's complete independence from king and ministry, was more than Newcastle could ever hope to get George II to agree to. On the other hand, no one dared accept the vacant positions without the approval of the prince. Thus the matter remained a stalemate until late in 1760 when, Prince George's twenty-first birthday having passed, he filled the vacancies without even warning the king.

Newcastle had tried hard to satisfy Bute, and he lost no opportunity to redeem himself. When Bute mentioned a minor post in the customs, which was disputed between two Cornish boroughs, the duke hastened to appoint Bute's nominee, even though it meant antagonizing a powerful local ally.[20] Again,

---

Bute, 3 December 1757, Lord Bolingbroke to Bute, Friday [November 1757?], Duke of Manchester to Bute, 6 February 1758, Bute MSS.

17. Pitt to Bute, Friday 7 o'clock [November-December 1757], Bute MSS.

18. Bute to Pitt [May, 1758], Bute MSS (copy); this letter is pub. in *Chatham Correspondence*, I, 170–71, where it is misdated 20 July 1756; punctuation and style indicate that the copy is more nearly accurate than the pub. version.

19. Pitt to Bute, Tuesday night [May 1758], Bute MSS, Sedgwick, "Pitt Letters," p. 144.

20. Newcastle to Bute, 8 February 1758, Bute MSS; for the background see Sir Lewis Namier, *The Structure of Politics at the Accession of George III*, 2nd ed. (London, 1957), p. 340.

when Bute demanded a Commissionership of the Excise for Prince George's former tutor, Newcastle gave it to him, despite the fact that he had already promised the position to one of his own relatives.[21] And when Pitt hinted that the earl wanted to place his brother in the vacant Ministry to Turin, Newcastle immediately recommended "the good consequences of it" to the king and secured the post for Mackenzie.[22] None of these favors earned Newcastle the least gratitude from Leicester House. Instead, Bute carped about delays and difficulties, and when he did assign any credit, gave it all to Pitt.[23]

Despite these repeated failures to ingratiate himself at Leicester House, Newcastle was determined to continue trying, for however often he might claim to be weary of office, the prospect of a new reign where he might be excluded from the government was terrifying to a man who had spent his entire adult life and much of his vast fortune in the struggle for power. Less than a month after securing the Ministry at Turin for Mackenzie, Newcastle was working on yet another request from Bute—this time that Prince Edward, second oldest of Princess Augusta's sons, should be permitted to join the navy as a volunteer.[24] Once again George II, on Newcastle's urging, granted the request, and once again the credit went to Pitt.[25]

Prince Edward did not make a great reputation for military prowess in his new role, but this was not important. There were considerably more substantial motives underlying Bute's desire to see him serving in the navy and on this particular ex-

21. Newcastle to Bute, 8 February 1758, Bute MSS.
22. Pitt to Bute, [29 May 1758], [31 May 1758], Bute MSS, Sedgwick, "Pitt Letters," pp. 148–49; Newcastle, "Memds. for the King," 2 June 1758, B.M. Add. MS. 32,880, f. 301.
23. For a fuller treatment of these appointments see McKelvey "Bute and George III," pp. 145–49.
24. Pitt to Bute, Wednesday past 6 o'clock [5 July 1758], Bute MSS, Sedgwick, "Pitt Letters," p. 155.
25. Bute to Pitt, [6 July 1758], *Chatham Correspondence*, I, 156–58 (misdated 3 June 1756).

pedition.²⁶ Leicester House was entering into an independent military policy of its own, based on the traditional opposition hatred of Hanover.

Bute had long been active in the field of military patronage. Despite George II's attempt to reform the purchase of commissions in the army there were still numerous favors that could be done by those in power. Commissions in new regiments, promotions, leaves, choice assignments (especially for naval officers)—all of these were eagerly sought by the friends and dependents of those with influence. Bute, anxious to oblige those who asked favors, usually forwarded their applications with his endorsement, and the ministers and officers to whom he sent them, equally anxious to oblige the prince's favorite, normally granted whatever was asked.²⁷

Far more important than this routine patronage was Bute's attempt to gain for Leicester House some control over the actual running of the war. The choice of the new commander-in-chief, Lord Ligonier, was known to have Bute's support, for the old general was expected to be much more amenable to the wishes of the heir than the Duke of Cumberland or one of his nominees would have been.

The British army in Germany was thoroughly infiltrated with friends of Leicester House. When the Duke of Marlborough transferred from the command of the British coastal forces to the command of all English forces serving under Prince Ferdinand in Germany, Lord George Sackville, Bute's disciple, went with him. When Marlborough died, Lord George succeeded as commander-in-chief of the British army in Germany.

Other friends of Leicester House received the prince's backing in obtaining high places in Ferdinand's army. Lord Downe, one of Prince George's few remaining Lords of the

26. For their concern on this point see Pitt to Bute, Monday past 11 [17 July 1758], Bute MSS, Sedgwick, "Pitt Letters," pp. 158–59.
27. Bute MSS, *ad passim.*

Bedchamber, was not only granted permission to join the army, but had Bute's active assistance in securing a lieutenant colonelcy and a regiment in Germany.[28] Colonel David Graeme, who had worked with Bute in negotiating a new "capitulation" for the Scotch-Dutch Brigade,[29] appeared in Germany as an unofficial observer—and as one of Bute's closest military advisers.[30] Leicester House was thus kept constantly informed of German events, and, once Sackville held the German command, Bute could even hope to influence the course of the continental war.

The prospect of amphibious attacks on the French coast was of even greater concern to Leicester House. These attacks had begun in 1757 as a means of easing French pressure in Germany and bolstering English morale. At Leicester House, however, they were viewed as much more—as an alternative, not an adjunct, to British involvement in Germany. However much Bute and the Prince of Wales might rejoice at the victories of Frederick the Great, they remained convinced that England should never have become involved in a Prussian alliance. Far better than fighting the French on the continent, in an expensive land war, was the utilization of what Bute called "the true palladium of this country, our naval power," in raids on the French coast. For the navy, "properly managed, under a Prince that knows its consequences, will ever keep Britain formidable without impoverishing it, and prove a surer means of humbling France, than any other whatever."[31] Bute continually reminded Pitt of Leicester House's preference for these raids as an alternative to greater involvement in Germany.[32] Furthermore, the less Britain was committed to continental allies, the easier it would be to bring the war to an

28. Downe to Bute, Bute MSS, 1758 *ad passim.*
29. See McKelvey, "Lord Bute and George III," pp. 152–53.
30. David Graeme to Bute, 15 November 1758, Bute MSS.
31. Bute to Pitt, 8 September 1758, *Chatham Correspondence,* I, 349–50.
32. *Ibid.*; Bute to Pitt, 2 July 1758, *Chatham Correspondence,* I, 323–24; Bute to Pitt, Friday 2 [Summer 1757], PRO 30/8/24, f. 327.

end—a goal very much desired by the Prince of Wales and Bute.[33]

It was this predilection for assaults on the French coast which led Leicester House to intervene decisively in military affairs in the summer of 1758. A large expedition, including some 13,000 troops and over 180 ships, had been prepared by Pitt for a major diversionary effort against the privateering port of St. Malo. When the fleet sailed in June, Bute was hopeful that its success would remove the pressure for additional British forces for Germany.[34] But when news arrived in London of the abandonment of the attempt on St. Malo, the earl told Pitt gloomily that he foresaw "where all this will end"— in yet greater continental entanglements.[35]

Bute was determined that this failure should not mean an end to expeditions. As soon as the fleet returned to Portsmouth, he wrote Pitt: "For God's sake, let their stay here be as brief as possible!" Bute feared that the officers would clamor to join the forces going to Germany, where a more conventional type of war was being fought.[36] If they were to succeed, Newcastle and the king might well seize the excuse to abandon the entire expeditionary approach, an approach which they had always disliked. This is the reason Bute suddenly urged that Prince Edward should join the expedition as a volunteer; his doing so would publicly demonstrate Leicester House support for coastal attacks.

The Duke of Marlborough, an officer of great estate but little ability, did manage to substitute the command of the forces destined for Emden for the command of the expedition, and Lord George Sackville, his second in command, went with him. Sackville's departure placed a new emphasis on the other

33. Prince of Wales to Bute, [circa 2 July 1758], Sedgwick, *Letters from George III*, pp. 10–11.
34. Bute to Pitt, Thursday night [8 June 1758], PRO 30/8/24, f. 308.
35. Bute to Pitt, [16 June 1758], *Chatham Correspondence*, I, 318–19.
36. Bute to Pitt, [2 July 1758], *Chatham Correspondence*, I, 323–24.

Leicester House supporters in the expeditionary force. Prince Edward, though his presence was useful as an indication of his brother's sympathies, could not be expected to have any part in making decisions. Neither General Bligh nor Lord Howe, the military and naval commanders, had ties with Leicester House. But there were other officers whose loyalty to Bute was unquestionable. Major General Elliot, who owed his transfer from the Dutch to the British army to Bute,[37] was serving in the expedition and was recognized as a highly competent officer.[38] Colonel Clerk, a Scot and a close friend of Bute's, was serving as quartermaster general, a position he had received on Bute's recommendation. Clerk was a born intriguer, and confident of his superiority to any commander he might serve under. He was also an enthusiastic supporter of coastal assaults.[39] It is thus logical, though unfortunate, that Bute chose Clerk to act as his personal representative on the expedition.

The fleet remained in harbor for over a month after the St. Malo fiasco and then sailed for the French coast on August 1. Cherbourg fell, but was abandoned after the port and fortifications were destroyed. Returning to England on August 19, the expedition again stayed in port until the last day of the month, when it left once more for France. During this interval between August 19 and August 31, the officers received no new orders, but plans were laid, nonetheless, for another attack on St. Malo. The inspiration for this plan came directly from Leicester House.

Clerk had begun urging Bligh and Howe to attack St. Malo as early as July,[40] and he succeeded in convincing them that St. Malo was the only objective that could restore public con-

37. General Elliot to Bute, 25 April 1758, Bute MSS.
38. Julian S. Corbett, *England in the Seven Years' War* (London, 1907), I, 294.
39. Dodington, *Diary*, p. 354.
40. Clerk to Bute, 27 July 1758, Bute MSS.

fidence in the expeditionary idea.⁴¹ There is no doubt that Bute originated this plan and that the objective for which the fleet sailed was fully known to Leicester House, though completely unknown to any of the ministers.⁴² Bute was convinced that only a successful conclusion to the 1758 campaigning season could save the strategy of coastal attacks, and he apparently thought that no other objective offered such great possibilities as St. Malo, the scene of an earlier failure. Once again his hopes were high. On August 25, anticipating the sailing of the fleet by almost a week, Bute wrote his agent in Scotland, William Mure, that "I should imagine the blow is striking now [which] will efface the infamy" of the earlier defeats.⁴³

Unfortunately, this final descent on the French coast was a total disaster. Though the prime characteristic of the expedition was confusion, two things were clear: the French were fully prepared for the attack, and both Bligh and Clerk were negligent in their duties. This is particularly true of Clerk, who failed at the crucial moment to make adequate arrangements for the safety of the troops.⁴⁴ Bute had made a serious error in his judgment of Clerk. He had repeatedly expressed his complete confidence in him, on one occasion telling Pitt that "never was a man so cut out for bold and hardy enterprises."⁴⁵ Though Bute, characteristically, never acknowledged his error, he now had to pay the price for his mistake—the St. Malo expedition was the last of its type, and Britain was drawn still deeper into the German war.

41. Clerk to Bute, 21 August 1758, Bute MSS.
42. *Ibid.*: "our course which you know;" Hardwicke to Newcastle, Saturday, 7 October 1758, B.M. Add. MS. 32,884, f. 290; Newcastle to Hardwicke, 5 October 1758, B.M. Add. MS. 32,884, f. 262.
43. Bute to William Mure, 28 August [1758], Mure, *Caldwell Papers*, II, 119.
44. On Clerk's incompetence see Corbett, *Seven Years' War*, I, 294ff.; *Gentlemen's Magazine*, XXVIII (1758), 534.
45. Bute to Pitt, 8 September 1758, *Chatham Correspondence*, I, 349–50; for Bute's high opinion of Clerk, see also Bute to William Mure, 25 August [1758], Mure, *Caldwell Papers*, II, 119.

## THE NEW ADMINISTRATION 73

Bute had gambled for high stakes, hoping that a successful expedition would forestall the Hanoverian tendencies of George II and Newcastle. He may even have entertained an idea of claiming credit for a victory at St. Malo—Lord Hardwicke thought that the presence of Prince Edward with the fleet indicated precisely that.[46] But now the gamble was lost, and Bute was faced with the problem of recovering what he could from the wreckage. His solution was indignant outrage. When the king forbade Bligh to appear at court, Bute sent an impassioned letter to Pitt. "Nothing," he wrote, "has ever happen'd; since We put the Crown once more, on that little Pelhams head; that so tho'rily opens my Eyes." Why was Bligh "to be singl'd out" for such harsh treatment, when he was the only man to win a victory on the French coast (Cherbourg)?[47] The answer, to Bute, was clear: the whole commotion was a "contrivance between the King, and the Duke of Newcastle, to cry down, and discredit, Expeditions," and to prevent the Prince of Wales from having any role in government.[48]

As Charles Jenkinson pointed out about the attack on Bligh and Clerk, "there is much of politics in this affair."[49] Hardwicke put the idea a bit strongly, but he correctly diagnosed Bute's fears when he wrote: "I question whether He [Bute] cares one farthing for Blighe, & perhaps not a halfpenny for Clarke; but it reflects some dishonour upon the Prince & the Adviser, & perhaps somebody or other might be tempted to blab who put them upon it."[50] Once it became clear that no one was going to "blab" Bute calmed down, although he

46. Hardwicke to Newcastle, 7 October 1758, B.M. Add. MS. 32,884, f. 290.
47. Bute to Pitt, Monday [25 September 1758], PRO 30/8/24, ff. 316–17 (inaccurately published in Sedgwick, "Pitt Letters," pp. 162–64).
48. Newcastle to Hardwicke, 5 October 1758, B.M. Add. MS. 32,884, f. 260.
49. Charles Jenkinson to George Grenville, 30 September 1758, *Grenville Papers*, I, 272.
50. Hardwicke to Newcastle, 7 October 1758, B.M. Add. MS. 32,884, f. 290.

was unwilling to forget the St. Malo fiasco altogether. Before the storm caused by Clerk's incompetence had even begun to subside, Bute wrote Pitt that "He should ask, and even *force*" the king to promote Clerk to a colonelcy of Marines.[51] When Pitt refused to do this, on the grounds that every officer in the army was violently opposed to Clerk, Bute appealed to Ligonier and Lord Barrington, the minister of war, on behalf of Lord Fitzmaurice, Clerk's protégé.[52] Both of these men were closely identified with the ill-fated Leicester House expeditionary policy, and Bute's failure to gain them promotions reinforced the earl's conviction that he and the prince were the victims of a pro-Hanoverian conspiracy. And it now began to appear to Bute that Pitt, though not perhaps a member of the conspiracy himself, was failing to forward the policies of Leicester House with any great vigor.

Certainly the relationship between Bute and Pitt was changing. Two factors underly this change: the realization that Cumberland was no longer a threat, and Pitt's gradual development of assurance in his office. For more than a year after the formation of the Pitt-Newcastle ministry, the secretary and the Groom of the Stole remained the closest of friends. In the summer of 1758, Bute still had "entire confidence" in Pitt,[53] and Pitt, in turn, praised Bute's judgment and benign influence over the Prince of Wales.[54] Once Prince Ferdinand's victories eliminated the possibility of Cumberland's recall, however, Pitt had less need for Leicester House support, and

---

51. "P.S." [Newcastle to Hardwicke], 17 October 1758, B.M. Add. MS. 32,884, f. 412.

52. Ligonier to Bute, 2 November 1758, Bute MSS; "C.V.," Newcastle House, 15 December 1758, B.M. Add. MS. 32,886, f. 326; Barrington to Bute, 4 December 1758, Bute MSS.

53. Bute to Pitt, 4 June 1758, *Chatham Correspondence*, I, 316–17. Bute was expressing similar sentiments as late as August: Bute to Pitt, Sunday [20 August 1758], *Chatham Correspondence*, I, 335–36.

54. Pitt to Bute, Tuesday 4 o'clock [20 June 1758], Bute MSS, Sedgwick, "Pitt Letters," p. 152.

Bute felt more free to ask Pitt's help in the everyday transactions of government. Their friendship had been born in the mutual interest of opposition, and once Pitt became an accepted member of George II's ministry, with his time and energy almost totally absorbed in the management of the war, Dodington's prediction to Prince Frederick—that no Leicester House politician could serve the king and remain a friend to the heir as well—seemed to come true.

Strains had begun to appear in their relationship long before any actual break could be seen. Each man had specific interests close to his heart: Pitt demanded an extension of habeas corpus; Bute was stubbornly set against British intervention in Germany. While each supported the other in public, neither of them could really understand the depth of the other's commitment.

Early in 1758 Pitt had drafted an act extending the right of habeas corpus to any man pressed into military service. Bute certainly led Pitt to believe that he supported the bill. When it was defeated in the House of Lords he bemoaned to Pitt "the total loss of public spirit, and the most supreme indifference to those valuable rights, for the obtaining of which our ancestors freely risked both life and fortune!"[55] Later he tried to connect the antiexpeditionary group with those who had opposed the Habeas Corpus Act.[56] These sentiments were for Pitt's reassurance only. In fact, Bute was little concerned with "those valuable rights," but he was afraid that Pitt's stubbornness might destroy the arduously built ministry. The earl made it clear to Newcastle and Hardwicke that Leicester House did not support the Habeas Corpus Act.[57]

If Bute was guilty of duplicity on habeas corpus, Pitt was

---

55. Bute to Pitt, 4 June 1758, *Chatham Correspondence*, I, 316–17.
56. Bute to Pitt, [25 September 1758], PRO 30/8/24, ff. 216–17.
57. Newcastle to Hardwicke, 21 May 1758, B.M. Add. MS. 32,880, f. 175; Newcastle, "Memds. for the King," 24 May 1758, B.M. Add. MS. 32,880, f. 216.

far from truthful on the issue of British troops for Germany. Early in 1758 Pitt had repeatedly assured the House of Commons that he would not send "a drop of our blood to the Elbe, to be lost in that ocean of gore."[58] When Pitt changed his mind, and recommended sending "some squadrons of English cavalry" to the Rhine, he reminded Bute that Leicester House had approved just such a small scale reinforcement.[59] Bute replied that he approved, but cautioned Pitt to keep a wary eye on his colleagues, "that a small body should not lead to a great one."[60]

Three days later, on June 26th, Pitt reaffirmed his agreement with Bute. "Be assured," he wrote, that "I will not be drawn further than my own conviction, authorised and confirmed by your concurrence shall suggest." But in the same letter Pitt announced that "some squadrons" had now become five regiments, "about 2,000 men."[61] Even this was far below the actual total. On June 24, George II, with Pitt's approval, had ordered 5,000 troops sent to Germany. And in less than two weeks the number had risen to 9,000.[62]

When Pitt's deception became clear, the Leicester House leaders were furious. Bute had approved of a small auxiliary force of cavalry as an assurance to Frederick the Great, but the end result was a major expedition of both cavalry and foot. Worse still, both officers and troops were taken from the coastal forces and sent to Germany—thus weakening the assault on St. Malo.[63] The spectre of full scale British involvement on the continent had now materialized, and Prince

58. Williams, *Pitt*, I, 355.
59. Pitt to Bute, [23 June 1758], Bute MSS, Sedgwick, "Pitt Letters," pp. 153–54.
60. Bute to Pitt, Friday past seven [23 June 1758], PRO 30/8/24, f. 329.
61. Pitt to Bute, Monday evening [26 June 1758], Bute MSS, Sedgwick, "Pitt Letters," pp. 154–55.
62. Williams, *Pitt*, I, 357.
63. This was not at all to the liking of Bute and the Prince: Bute to Pitt, [2 July 1758], *Chatham Correspondence*, I, 323–24.

George and Bute fumed at the duplicity of their "wavering friend."[64]

As long as there was still hope for the St. Malo expedition, Bute suppressed his anger, but when the assault failed and Bligh was barred from court, Bute's wrath came into the open. Twice during October he denounced Pitt for reversing his stand on German intervention,[65] and Count Viry reported that Bute was displeased with Pitt for other reasons as well. Pitt, the earl felt, "had too much Regard" for Newcastle, and "gave up all Recommendations to Employments &c" to him.[66] Furthermore, Pitt was too skimpy in his reports to Leicester House, in marked contrast to the other secretary of state, Lord Holdernesse, who was courting Bute's favor by sending him "the most minute Accounts that can be collected."[67] Bute, with some justification, felt that Pitt was not fulfilling the role which Leicester House had anticipated for him—he gave Newcastle too much authority in appointments, he had retreated from his stand on continental intervention, and he was not even keeping Bute and the prince adequately informed. The heir and his adherents were simply not enjoying the influence in the government which they had expected.

In an attempt at reconciliation, Bute and Pitt met in early October. The former repeated his attacks on the administration's continental policy and condemned close collaboration with Newcastle. Pitt justified himself on both points and then questioned Bute's growing friendship with Bubb Dodington, who was entirely "a Friend to the Duke of Cumberland, & Mr.

64. Prince of Wales to Bute, [circa 2 July 1758], Sedgwick, *Letters from George III*, pp. 10–11.
65. [Newcastle to Hardwicke], 10 October 1758, 31 October 1758, B.M. Add. MSS 32,884, f. 312; 32,885, ff. 153–54.
66. Newcastle to Hardwicke, Friday morning [6 October 1758], B.M. Add. MS. 32,884, f. 265.
67. *Ibid.*; for an example see Holdernesse to Bute, 27 June 1758, and Pitt to Bute, 27 June 1758, Bute MSS.

Fox."[68] Bute was, in fact, encouraging Dodington in order to show that Leicester House had other alternatives, that they were even willing to consider an alliance with Fox's faction.[69] Despite this irritant Bute and Pitt "parted civilly," although Count Viry reported that Pitt and the whole Grenville clan were "not well" with Bute.[70] Certainly the meeting failed to satisfy Bute, who reiterated the same complaints about Pitt several times in the next two months.[71]

Dodington could be treated as a momentary aberration; the same was not true of Legge. Pitt had hated the chancellor of the Exchequer ever since Legge's independent negotiations with Newcastle in the spring of 1755, and so long as Pitt and Bute remained on good terms Bute did little to encourage Legge, though he felt no particular animosity toward him.[72] But after St. Malo, "Lord B. began to be fonder of . . . Legge; and to talk of His Abilities & cool Judgement, rather in preference to Mr. Pitt."[73] By the middle of December, 1758, Count Viry could report to Newcastle that "Mr. Pitt, & the Grenvilles, hate Legge worse than Fox; but that Lord Bute will support Legge, in spite of them."[74] Bute could have done nothing which would have annoyed Pitt more.

Pitt's friends could be irritating too, especially his brother-in-law, Lord Temple. Though Temple was probably the least likeable of the whole Pitt-Grenville connection, he had been

---

68. [Newcastle to Hardwicke], 10 October 1758, B.M. Add. MS. 32,884, ff. 312–13.

69. Newcastle to Hardwicke, 5 October 1758, B.M. Add. MS. 32,884, f. 263.

70. [Newcastle to Hardwicke], 10 October 1758, B.M. Add. MS. 32,884, ff. 312–13.

71. [Newcastle to Hardwicke], 31 October 1758, B.M. Add. MS. 32,885, ff. 153–54.

72. Newcastle to Hardwicke, 7 January 1758, B.M. Add. MS. 32,877, f. 50.

73. [Newcastle to Hardwicke], 31 October 1758, B.M. Add. MS. 32,885, ff. 153–54.

74. "C.V. Private," Newcastle House, 19 December 1758, B.M. Add. MS. 32,886, ff. 384–86.

well received at Leicester House in the early part of 1758.[75] But after St. Malo all of the Grenvilles fell from favor with the prince, and Temple felt the full force of Bute's anger when he asked the king for a Garter the princess thought should go to her own son, Prince William.[76]

Difficulties with Temple, Legge, or Dodington were merely peripheral; they could not obscure the major disagreement between Bute and Pitt, which was renewed in December by Pitt's support for increased British funds for Germany and by his continued failure to notify Leicester House of policy decisions.[77] Pitt was not yet ready to abandon his connection with the Prince of Wales altogether, and he sought a meeting with Bute in an attempt to straighten out their problems. The German question was no longer the primary issue discussed, perhaps because Bute had despaired of regaining Pitt's cooperation in this sphere. The conversation centered on Pitt's "reservedness" in keeping the prince informed and on the position of Newcastle after the accession.[78] The first was passed over after Pitt defended himself by stating that Holdernesse kept the prince informed of all the details anyway. The second issue was more basic. Pitt's vacillation had compelled a rethinking of future policy at Leicester House. So long as the chief power in the ministry had been closely identified with the heir, there was no real problem, but once Pitt's loyalty had become questionable Bute demanded reassurance. He did not obtain any. Pitt stated firmly that "in case of an Accident to the King . . . . Every Thing should be

75. Countess Temple to Earl Temple, 13 May [1758], *Grenville Papers*, I, 237.
76. [Newcastle to Hardwicke], 14 November 1758, B.M. Add. MS. 32,885, f. 324.
77. Prince of Wales to Bute, [*circa* 8 December 1758], Sedgwick, *Letters from George III*, p. 18.
78. "C.V. Private," Newcastle House, 19 December 1758, B.M. Add. MS. 32,886, ff. 384–86.

done, in Concert with the Duke of Newcastle."[79] Bute refused to accept this idea: "to be Minister of this Country hereafter, was what the Duke of Newcastle could not be."[80] Despite the lack of agreement, Viry reported that "They parted well; And all seems made up"; but he added a cautionary "for the present."[81]

Certainly no permanent reconciliation resulted. Both Pitt and Bute were reluctant, however, to end their relationship, if only because of the satisfaction which that would give to their enemies.[82] The Prince of Wales was more rash. He was certain that Pitt had "given himself either up to the K. or the D. of N. or else he could not act the infamous and ungrateful part he now does."[83] "Indeed," he wrote Bute, "he treats both you and me with no more regard than he would a parcel of children, he seems to forget that the day will come, when he must expect to be treated according to his deserts."[84]

Pitt and Bute continued to communicate with one another occasionally in 1759, and they even cooperated in some minor matters, but all warmth between them was dead. It is unlikely that their friendship could have been long maintained in any case. The role which Bute envisioned for Pitt, as the prince's glorified errand boy in the king's government, was one Pitt could never have filled. He was concerned with the realities of power rather than with the lesser questions of prestige and patronage which dominated the thinking of Bute. But beyond these political differences lay a fundamental conflict of per-

79. *Ibid.*
80. "C.V. Private," Newcastle House, 20 December 1758, B.M. Add. MS. 32,886, f. 411.
81. "C.V. Private," Newcastle House, 19 December 1758, B.M. Add. MS. 32,886, ff. 384–86.
82. "C.V. Private," Newcastle House, 20 December 1758, B.M. Add. MS. 32,886, f. 411.
83. Prince of Wales to Bute, 9 o'clock [December 1758], Sedgwick, *Letters from George III*, p. 19.
84. Prince of Wales to Bute, past ten [*circa* 8 December 1758], Sedgwick, *Letters from George III*, p. 18.

sonality. Each of them had a grandiose notion of his own importance; neither could really stand to see the other in the first position. Lord Hardwicke summed up the situation well when he wrote, "I have allways been of opinion that Jealousies & Distrusts would arise between Lord B. and Mr. Secretary.... I should guess that it proceeds very much from want of Communication on the part of the latter, to which his reserve, & being so much shut up, together with some Contempt of other People's understandings, greatly disposed him."[85] He could, with equal justice, have said just about the same thing of Bute.

---

85. Hardwicke to Newcastle, 7 October 1758, B.M. Add. MS. 32,884, f. 290.

## SIX

## THE PRINCE AND
## HIS FAVORITE

If the Prince of Wales was upset by the break with Pitt, he was horrified by the subsequent suggestion that he should now abandon his plan for making Bute first lord of the Treasury in a new reign. By September, 1758, Prince George had become so dependent on Bute that he could not envision accepting the throne without the counsel of his "dearest friend." "If you shall ever think fit to take this step," he wrote,

> my line of action is plain; for though I act wrong in perhaps most things, yet I have too much spirit to accept the Crown and be a sypher, and too much love for my countrymen to mount this throne and be their detestation, I would therefore in such an unhappy case retire to some distant region where in solitude I might for the rest of my life remain, and think on the various faults I have committed . . .[1]

In December, when Bute repeated his idea of abstaining from office, Prince George replied that he saw "with horror ... the inevitable mischiefs that would arise from your taking such a step."[2] Bute remained reluctant, and the prince became still more abject. "Tis too much for mortal man to bear," he wrote. "I should look upon it as the greatest instance of your

---

1. Prince of Wales to Bute, 25 September 1758, Sedgwick, *Letters from George III*, pp. 13-14.
2. The quotations in this paragraph are all taken from Prince George's letters to Bute in December, 1758, Sedgwick, *Letters from George III*, pp. 18-22.

friendship if you would tell me what it is in me that makes you so extremely doubtful of accepting the office you yourself consented to two years ago, that I might convince you that you may with safety rely on my conduct." Soon this theme of self-abasement became even stronger: "I don't deny that the scene looks very black; ... I will frankly own that through the negligence, if not wickedness of those around me in my earlier days, and since perhaps through my own indolence of temper, I have not that degree of knowledge and experience in business, one of my age might reasonably have acquir'd," but how much worse off must he be if he could not count on Bute's "holesome advice?" Bute finally agreed to reconsider, and the young prince was rapturous; nothing could fill his "heart with greater joy," he wrote.

As this episode shows, the immature and neurotic prince had become completely dependent on Bute. Nothing is more illustrative of the relationship between the two than the prince's tentative approaches to telling Bute of his love for Lady Sarah Lennox, his infantile gushing when he finally did so, and his abject retreat from the idea of marrying her as soon as the earl told him that the marriage of the heir apparent to an Englishwoman was unthinkable.[3] But Bute did more than just direct the prince in his major decisions. He also supervised the everyday affairs of his life and his court. It was Bute who chose Prince George's reading, who instructed him on the proper way of addressing the various classes of his subjects, and who urged him to gain "innocent popularity" from his future subjects by attending plays and the opera.[4]

This dependence was based on adoration and self-abasement. The prince had a very high opinion of Bute, and a very low opinion of himself. Certainly it was an unusual young man of twenty who could write that he was "deeply afflicted

3. Sedgwick, *Letters from George III*, pp. 35-39.
4. Bute to the Prince of Wales, [1756?], B.M. Add. MS. 36,797, f. 67 (copy).

at the many things" Bute had told him the night before; "they have set me in a most dreadful light before my own eyes. I now see plainly that I have been my greatest enemy; for had I always acted according to your advice, I should now have been the direct opposite from what I am; nothing but the true love you bear me, could have led you to remain with me so long."[5] And two years later, when Bute again pointed out his numerous faults, the prince meekly replied that "nothing can be more friendly than your constant endeavours to point out those things in me that are likely to destroy any attempts of raising my character."[6]

Bute's influence over the prince had grown rapidly since 1755, when the princess dowager had entrusted the eduction of her "backward" son to the Scottish earl. Bute had accepted this task with "all the warmth that duty, gratitude and friendship can inspire,"[7] and during the following years he spent much of his time and energy directing the prince's studies. Bute achieved remarkable success—a success that can be seen in the improvement of the prince's spelling and grammar and in his steadily growing knowledge of history and constitutional theory.

The Whig historians of the nineteenth century frequently claimed that George III had been educated in "unconstitutional" notions of British government. It is now clear that Sir Lewis Namier and Romney Sedgwick were correct when they claimed that George III's ideas were, in a strict sense, "constitutional," but in a period where the constitution was highly fluid, the term by itself does not mean much. One constitutional authority definitely known to have been included in the prince's education was Blackstone,[8] who favored a broad interpreta-

    5. Prince of Wales to Bute, 25 September 1758, Sedgwick, *Letters from George III*, pp. 13–14.
    6. Prince of Wales to Bute, 4 May 1760, Sedgwick, *Letters from George III*, pp. 44–46.
    7. Bute to Princess of Wales, [1755], B.M. Add. MS. 36,797, f. 69 (copy).
    8. William Blackstone to Bute, 15 March 1759, Bute MSS.

tion of the royal prerogative. Lord Bute and the Prince of Wales shared this bias. Once, after receiving some of Blackstone's lectures in manuscript, the earl told Lord Lincoln that he "lamented the paring down the prerogative, & the low state to which the House of Lords were at present reduced,"[9] and Prince George echoed virtually the same idea.[10]

Whether or not the prince was educated in a "constitutional" manner, what is important is that the heir to the throne did absorb and accept a definite set of political beliefs which he then attempted to put into practice upon his accession. There is an unpublished document preserved in the Bute Manuscripts which is, in effect, a prospectus for the instruction of the prince.[11] Prince George's complete acceptance of the ideas presented in this paper, and the fact that he based many of his later actions on them, shows how successful Bute's pedagogy was, and how far reaching its consequences were to be.

The dominant theme of this document is the pernicious influence of faction. The author states that both Whigs and Tories had concurred in the Hanoverian Succession, but the Whigs "made the greatest noise, pretended the greatest zeal, and assumed the sole merit." They thus captured George I and "made the late King their instrument for the good of their faction." Everyone not of this faction was "to be exterminated." Consequently the realm was in grave danger of being divided and destroyed by the triumphant faction, drunk with power, and the defeated faction, made desperate by persecution. This was the true origin of the madness that caused the Jacobite rebellions of 1715 and 1745.

Before the end of his reign George I came to realize the

9. Newcastle, "Memds. for My Lord Lincoln," 18 March 1759, B.M. Add. MS. 32,889, f. 137.
10. Prince of Wales, "Thoughts on the British Constitution," Bute Corresp.
11. This document is unsigned and is not in Bute's hand, but it can be dated on internal evidence as falling in either 1755 or early 1756, and the ideas in it are so consistent with those advocated by Bute that it seems safe to assume that either he was the author or that someone else wrote it under his direction.

mistake he had made, "of the power he had suffered a cabal to assume; by which they had tyrannized the nation, and, in many instances, even himself." If the king had only lived a little longer, "we might have seen a coalited, that is a national party formed." But he died before this could happen, and the "national party," instead of controlling the government, became the opposition under George II. Walpole and his henchmen were able to continue their stranglehold on the government through corruption, military force, and the "intrigues and influence of Queen Caroline."

If this system continued into a third reign, it would be "fatal to the nation, and to a future King." It was, therefore, essential that the next sovereign reform the abuses which had almost destroyed Great Britain. So far had the nation sunk into selfishness and faction that reform would not be easy; decades of Whig rule had brought the country to the brink of bankruptcy and foolish foreign policies had left Britain isolated and friendless.

"The result of this whole representation is this—Whenever the Prince of Wales succeeds to the crown, he will find the Kingdom poorer, and more exposed," than ever before in history. Only "the wisdom of the wisest and the courage of the bravest princes" can save him and his poor country. Fortunately, the prince will enjoy some advantages. "He is not a foreigner, but a prince born and bred in the country; . . . He will not have dipped in any faction, nor have rendered himself odious to any part of the nation from the Orcades down to the south of Britain. He will have no predilection for any other country [i.e. Hanover], nor any prejudices of foreign politics." Furthermore, "the universal esteem and affection for his Royal Mother, which runs thro the nation, will reflect some of it's lustre upon him, and prepare mankind to ascribe the same character to him, and to expect their political salvation from his government."

## THE PRINCE AND HIS FAVORITE    87

Two features of this presentation are distinctively Bute's: the consistent use of "Britain" or "British" instead of "England" or "English," and the flattery to Princess Augusta. The other points make up the traditional Leicester House program. The idea that the Whigs had seized control of the king and his ministry, and then run the government for their own benefit, was necessarily a key complaint raised by every group that hoped to replace those Whigs in power. This contention leads logically to the appeal for a "national party" instead of domination by "faction." Frugality, a forceful foreign policy and opposition to corruption, while not necessarily consistent, were always popular. And the emphasis on the prince's English birth and background, coupled with the denunciation of Hanover, served to point up the contrast between the situations of the first two Hanoverians and the heir apparent.

Traditional and recurrent though these themes may have been in eighteenth century oppositions, they were the mainstay of the prince's education, and there is every reason to believe that he accepted all of them as completely true. To the young prince they were not merely "flapdoodle," as Sir Lewis Namier has called them, but the essential principles on which he attempted to build his government.[12]

One other aspect of the prince's education must be mentioned. This is the stress placed on religious piety. George III's religion was very real. Even Lord Waldegrave, in his unflattering portrait of the prince when he was twenty, acknowledged that "his religion is free from all hypocrisy," though he added that it "is not of the most charitable sort."[13] Prince George had an abiding belief in the intervention of God in secular affairs, as this 1758 letter to Bute shows:

> I fear this check will prevent Gen. Abercrombie's pushing towards Crown Point; but in this as well as every

12. Namier, *England*, p. 84.    13. Waldegrave, *Memoirs*, p. 8.

thing else I entirely rely on the Almighty who knows best what is fit for us; the assistance he has given us at Louisburgh makes me hope we shall receive further marks of His goodness; I am certain that by trusting in Him; and attempting with Vigour to restore religion and virtue when I mount the throne this great country will probably regain her antient state of lustre.[14]

George's religious views were virtually identical to those held by Bute. The earl constantly emphasized the need for religious faith in an evil world. When Princess Elizabeth died in September, 1759, Bute wrote her bereaved brother that the loss was great,

> but you have advantages to bear it that few of your age, still fewer of your rank, enjoy. Accustomed from your childhood to look up to Heaven, you can in the day of affliction put full confidence in Him who gives and resumes at pleasure; . . . tis infinite consolation, Sir, to be able to take fast hold on our great Creator, our best Preserver, in all the good or bad that happens to us; to have our souls so pure, our consciences so free, that opprest with misery we may at once fly to Him . . .[15]

One final example, taken from a letter written by the prince to Bute in June, 1760, when Bute's daughter was gravely ill, will suffice to show the type of religious conviction which they shared:

> When I consider my Dearest Friend is an eye witness of whatever is in the womb of fate, I tremble lest he should be attacked with this distemper; in short my Dearest Friend my only comfort in this state of things is, the

---

14. Prince of Wales to Bute, Near 11 [20 August 1758], Sedgwick, *Letters from George III*, pp. 12–13.

15. Bute to the Prince of Wales, Friday morn, past ten [7 September 1759], Windsor Archives, Sedgwick, *Letters from George III*, p. 31.

knowing of your worth, and that you from your upright
conduct have some right to hope for particular assistance
from the great Author of us all . . ."[16]

Both Bute and the prince were convinced not only of the
existence of a personal and all powerful diety, but of their
righteousness in His eyes. Their policies and their ideas were
therefore sanctified by divine grace, and those who opposed
them must necessarily be both wrong and wicked.

This attitude could easily produce a conviction of persecution. In June, 1756, when George II was blocking Bute's promotion to Groom of the Stole, Prince George had written the earl that "My Friend is also attacked in the most cruel and horrid manner, not for anything he has done against them, but because he is my friend, and wants to see me come to the throne with honor and not with disgrace and because he is a friend to the bless'd liberties of his country and not to arbitrary notions."[17] And in April, 1760, Bute wrote Lord Talbot complaining of the ill usage he had received because of his friendship for Lord George Sackville. He did not mind, he said, the assault which the politicians made on his honor and reputation, for "'tis the Young Prince they Hate, 'tis his virtuous character they tremble for; the Heir of the Crown not to Encourage vice is Terrible!"[18]

Coupled with this sense of their own righteousness, Bute and the prince developed a growing contempt for all politicians. Pitt and the Grenvilles had demonstrated the faithlessness of that breed. "When I consider the cabals, & conduct of those who pretend to be Your Friends & Mine," wrote the prince in April, 1759, "I cannot help thinking they are Wolves

---

16. Prince of Wales to Bute, [June 1760], Sedgwick, *Letters from George III*, pp. 46–47.
17. Prince of Wales to Bute, 31 [sic] June 1756, Sedgwick, *Letters from George III*, pp. 2–4.
18. [Bute to Talbot], 23 April 1760, Bute Corresp. (draft).

in Sheeps Skins, & that any other set of men are as honest (or more properly) not dishonester."[19] Lack of honesty among politicians became a constant theme with the prince. "As to honesty, I think all sets of men seem equally to have thrown that aside" he wrote in December, 1758.[20] A year and a half later, he was still harping on the same idea: "for as to honesty, I have already lived long enough to know you [Bute] are the only man I shall ever meet with who possesses that quality."[21]

The prince had undoubtedly benefitted in many ways from the influence of Bute. By 1759 he was immeasurably better educated than he had been in 1755. His increasing knowledge, however, had not produced a corresponding maturity. At twenty he was still essentially the same moody and petulant youth that he had been five years before, but with the important difference that now he was convinced that he and his dearest friend shared a mission, no less a one than saving Britain from imminent ruin. Only with this background of immaturity and righteous zeal in mind is it possible to understand the depth of the prince's bitterness at the "desertion" of Pitt and the "faithless band" of Grenvilles.[22]

These attitudes were reflected in the political maneuvering at Leicester House in the early months of 1759. During this period Pitt dropped from favor. Legge correspondingly rose, Fox and his party were encouraged, and the Duke of Newcastle was vigorously courted. All of this was the result of the prince's disenchantment with politicians and his resulting determination, encouraged by Bute, to use them simply as "tools" in furthering the ends of Leicester House. There was a specific purpose behind each of these maneuvers. Pitt had

19. Prince of Wales to Bute, [April 1759?], Bute Corresp.
20. Prince of Wales to Bute, 9 o'clock [December 1758], Sedgwick, *Letters from George III*, pp. 18–19.
21. Prince of Wales to Bute, ½ hour past nine [23 April 1760], Sedgwick, *Letters from George III*, p. 43.
22. Prince of Wales to Bute, [circa 16 November 1759], Sedgwick, *Letters from George III*, p. 34.

to be chastised to show that no man could afford to be derelict in his duty to the prince. Legge was shown favor to indicate that Bute and the prince had other resources beyond Pitt. As Count Viry pointed out, "the more Mr. Pitt ran at Mr. Legge for his Behaviour, the more He recommended Legge to the Prince of Wales, and the fonder the Prince of Wales grew of Him."[23] Fox was encouraged in order to frighten the rest, and Newcastle was deluded into thinking himself a favorite of the prince because Bute wanted some concessions from the king which the duke was best qualified to gain.

The channel which Bute used to communicate the varying political trends at Leicester House was Count Viry, the Sardinian ambassador. Viry knew all of the important figures in London and was trusted—to a point—by all of them. Bute was well aware that what he said to Viry in the morning would be reported to the Duke of Newcastle the same afternoon and be common gossip within a few days. This made Viry a very useful means of making public whatever Bute wished to be thought about the inner workings of the heir's court.

The supposed rise of Fox at Leicester House is a good example. In January, 1759, Viry told Newcastle that Cumberland and Fox were making "great Advances" to Leicester House; on March 14 that "Leicester House had the greatest Offers," from Fox; and two days later that Cumberland was making "strong overtures" to the Prince of Wales through conversations between Princess Amelia and the princess dowager.[24] Finally, on the eve of Bute's temporary *rapprochement* with Newcastle in April, the ambassador told the Duke that Leicester House "had put an End entirely to all Negotiation, & Application, from a certain Quarter."[25] It is impossible to

23. "C.V.," Newcastle House, 21 February 1759, B.M. Add. MS. 32,888, ff. 204–5.
24. "C.V.," Newcastle House, 17 January 1759; 14 March 1759; 16 March 1759, B.M. Add. MSS 32,887, f. 205, 32,889, ff. 64–66, 103.
25. "C.V.," Newcastle House, 3 April 1759, B.M. Add. 32,889, ff. 348–49.

tell how much truth there is in all this, but it is clear that these rumors served to keep the situation fluid and Newcastle anxious, which was undoubtedly their purpose.

The declining fortunes of Pitt were also recorded in Viry's reports to Newcastle. In February the duke noted that Viry had told him of Bute's anger over the secretary's attacks on Legge's financial measures and that Bute had said "Mr. Pitt was not contented to be Secretary of State, but He must direct the Treasury too; which He ought not to do."[26] A month later, when Pitt wanted to improve his position at Leicester House, he used Viry as an intermediary, after complaining to the Sardinian that "They were reserv'd towards Him, and did not Speak to Him." Pitt added, however, that if Bute and the prince would only "let Him know their Sentiments, there was Nothing, He, (Pitt) would not do, to please them."[27]

As a result of Viry's intercession Pitt and Bute met on March 15. The secretary repeated his desire to conciliate Bute and the prince if they would only inform him of what was expected.[28] Nothing came of this meeting and two days later Viry told Newcastle that Princess Augusta was highly indignant at the way Pitt was treating his superior, the first lord of the Treasury.[29] This is, on the face of it, an incredible statement; Augusta certainly was not concerned about the welfare of the Duke of Newcastle. The date of this intelligence is significant, however, for on the next day, March 18, Bute met Lord Lincoln, Newcastle's nephew, and "expressed a great Desire on the Part of the Prince of Wales" for the friendship of the duke and his friends.[30]

26. "C.V.," Newcastle House, 21 February 1759, B.M. Add. MS. 32,888, ff. 204–5.
27. "C.V.," Newcastle House, 14 March 1759, B.M. Add. MS. 32,889, ff. 64–66.
28. "C.V.," Newcastle House, 16 March 1759, B.M. Add. MS. 32,889, ff. 100–2.
29. "C.V.," Newcastle House, 17 March 1759, B.M. Add. MS. 32,889, f. 121.
30. Newcastle, "Memds. for My Lord Lincoln," 18 March 1759, B.M. Add. MS. 32,889, ff. 136–37.

Bute had been preparing for this move for some time. His reputed dealings with Fox helped put Newcastle in a receptive frame of mind, and the suggestion that Pitt should not meddle in Treasury business was an obvious appeal to Newcastle's jealousy of the Great Commoner. On March 17 Bute had told Viry, for Newcastle's benefit, that the prince and princess were highly pleased with the duke for not interfering when an abortive attempt was made to renew the Brunswick marriage plans.[31]

All of this helped make Newcastle receptive to the overture from Leicester House. Lincoln told his uncle that Bute was concerned over "what Part the Duke of Newcastle & His Friends would take, In case of the Demise of the Crown," and that the earl had shown "a great Inclination to have a Connection, & Assurance from" the duke, the implication being that Bute would then be able to break off his negotiations with Fox.[32] Newcastle instructed Lincoln to reply to Bute that he had no desire "to undergo the Fatigue and Trouble of a Minister" in a new reign, but that he and his friends would "have nothing more at heart, than, . . . to support His Royal Highness's Government, and to prevent His Being overruled, or constrained by any Faction, or Combination of Men Whatsoever."[33]

After forty years of continuous government service, Newcastle may really have thought that he would enjoy retirement. Whether this was self-delusion or not is unimportant, for his answer was highly acceptable to Bute, who received the message from Lord Lincoln "with the utmost pleasure, & satisfaction." He then added that, although the duke "might think of declining the Trouble, & Fatigue of a Minister, He should be the most unhappy of all men, If He did not see" Newcastle

---

31. "C.V.," Newcastle House, 17 March 1759, B.M. Add. MS. 32,889, f. 124.
32. Newcastle, "Memds. for My Lord Lincoln," 18 March 1759, B.M. Add. MS. 32,889, ff. 136-37.
33. Newcastle, "Answer," B.M. Add. MS. 32,889, ff. 136-37.

and Hardwicke "at the Head of the Councils, & in the greatest Confidence with the Prince." Bute emphasized that he would do all in his power to give Newcastle "ease" in his present situation. The earl "repeated to My Lord Lincoln, His great desire of cultivating the D. of N., My Lord Hardwicke, & Their Friends. The Prince of Wales," said Bute, "knew the obligation the King's family had to them, that the P. of W. was a prince of a Grave & serious Turn, & would know how to distinguish, & take the advice of Men who had *Experience*, & Ability."[34] In the weeks that followed Bute built upon this opening,[35] with such great success that, by early April, Newcastle believed it when Bute told him that the Prince of Wales "look'd upon me, & My Friends, as His best Friends."[36]

One reason underlying this cultivation of Newcastle became apparent on April 11, when Bute called on the duke "and made a most reasonable Proposal from the Prince of Wales, to be submitted to the King." Now that the Prince of Wales was approaching his twenty-first birthday, Augusta felt that it was time for a separate establishment to be made for his younger brothers, along the same lines as that already created for Prince Edward.[37] Newcastle, basking in the good will of Leicester House, immediately presented the request to George II.[38]

Despite some minor problems which delayed the completion of the new establishment,[39] an unparalleled atmosphere of friendliness still prevailed. On April 29, at the King's Drawing Room, George II actually spoke to the Prince of Wales twice, "& the Conversation seemed to be particularly easy and in

34. Newcastle, "Substance of what passed between my Ld L & my Ld B," 21 March 1759, B.M. Add. MS. 32,889, f. 185–87.
35. McKelvey, "Bute and George III," pp. 199–200.
36. Newcastle, "A Short Account of What pass'd in My Conversation with My Lord Bute," 11 April 1759, B.M. Add. MS. 32,890, f. 11.
37. *Ibid.*, ff. 10–13.
38. Newcastle to Bute, 11 April 1759, Bute MSS.
39. McKelvey, "Bute and George III,' pp. 201–2.

good humour."[40] Two weeks later Bute invited Newcastle, Hardwicke and all their close associates to dinner—a dinner which Newcastle viewed as a "Publick Declaration" of Leicester House support.[41] The duke's euphoria was increased still further when he and Hardwicke celebrated the prince's birthday by dining again with Bute on June 4.[42]

Prince George's twenty-first birthday meant that he was now legally of age, and thus free from the direct control of his grandfather. Appointments to his household no longer required George II's approval, and his allowance, previously at the pleasure of the king, was now to be formally settled on him. Difficulties later arose over this last point,[43] but for the time being Bute and the prince were careful not to stir up any trouble, for they had still further objectives in mind.

Now that the prince was of age, both he and his favorite thought that he should take a more active role in public affairs. The specific sphere which they chose was disclosed on July 20th when Lord Pembroke delivered a letter from Prince George to the king. The prince wrote that "while this Country remain'd in Tranquillity, I thought my Time best employ'd, in acquiring a thorough Knowledge of all Matters, particularly suited to my Situation: But now that Every Part of the Nation is arming for It's Defence, I cannot bear the Thought of continuing in this inactive State."[44] Numerous compliments on the king's "Known Valour" and "accustom'd Goodness" followed, and it was only on a careful reading that it became clear that the prince desired a military appointment.

George II's reaction to the letter was predictable: assuming

40. Hardwicke to Newcastle, 29 April 1759, B.M. Add. MS. 32,890, f. 388.
41. Bute to Newcastle, 4 May 1759, B.M. Add. MS. 32,890, f. 476; Newcastle to Hardwicke, 6 May 1759, B.M. Add. MS. 32,891, ff. 5–6.
42. Newcastle to Hardwicke, 3 June 1759, B.M. Add. MS. 32,891, f. 402.
43. George II pared the allowance down to £35,000, and the prince considered this totally insufficient. See McKelvey, "Bute and George III," p. 204.
44. Prince of Wales to George II, 20 July 1759, B.M. Add. MS. 32,893, ff. 154–55 (copy).

that the prince wanted the "Command in Chief," he saw the request as an attempt to increase the prestige of the heir at the expense of the monarch. "He wants to be rising"; the king told Newcastle, *"monter un pas."*[45] George II's first impulse was to call in Pembroke and return an answer immediately, to the effect that "the Time was not yet come; that the case [presumably an invasion] did not yet exist."[46] Newcastle forsaw all of the good will of the spring disappearing at once and managed to convince the king that it would be best to wait and consider a proper reply.[47]

Newcastle turned to Hardwicke for advice. The former lord chancellor agreed with Newcastle that the cause of the letter was fear of the Duke of Cumberland's being named to the command in case of an invasion, but he added, "I go a little further & think that the Advisers of it do not expect an answer of agreement on His Majesty's part; but rather that the P. of W.'s having made such an offer, if it is not accepted, may make it more difficult to bring the Duke into that Situation." Hardwicke also noted that "this Measure seems to me to have been copied from the Step, which the Late Pr. of W. took in 1745, before the Duke was sent into Scotland, when He sent for Your Grace, Lord Harrington, & my self, seperately, & employed us all three to press the King that he might be sent to command the Forces in Scotland against the Rebels."[48]

Several days passed without a reply and Bute delegated his cousin, Lady Mary Coke, an intimate of the palace, to discover the cause of the delay. On July 25th Lady Mary found that no one knew anything of the prince's letter except Newcastle and the king. "You will be surprised," she wrote Bute, "to hear that my friends [Pitt and Holdernesse] knew Nothing of the Affair You Mentioned, nor has anybody been consulted but

45. Newcastle to Hardwicke, [20 July 1759], B.M. Add. MS. 32,893, ff. 172–73.
46. *Ibid.*
47. *Ibid.*
48. Hardwicke to Newcastle, 21 July 1759, B.M. Add. MS. 32,893, f. 202.

that Wretch the D—— of N——." She had informed both Pitt and Holdernesse and on the basis of their reactions she thought that everyone was "well inclined" except Newcastle.[49]

The duke was doing the best he could. It took him six days, but he finally got George II to agree that a committee of Newcastle, Pitt and Holdernesse should draw up an answer.[50] Newcastle was not, however, pushing the request itself with any vigor, presumably because he and Hardwicke assumed that the application was not in fact a serious one.[51] Convinced by Lady Mary that he could expect no help from Newcastle, Bute turned to Pitt. On July 26 he expressed to the secretary his amazement that no one had told him of the prince's request until Lady Mary had spoken to him on the 25th. "I wish," he continued, that "the Princes patience may hold out, in all these repeated scenes of neglect; he has been in the utmost anxiety for this week past, and with great difficulty deffered waiting on His Majesty in person." Bute enclosed a copy of the prince's letter, and concluded with the observation that, fearing "the consequences of a refusal, I make no doubt, but my worthy Friend, will see the propriety, I had almost said necessity of indulging His Royal Highness in so noble and reasonable a request, and that he will as far as the circumstances of his situation permit endeavour to procure it a favourable answer."[52]

The Prince of Wales reluctantly approved Bute's letter to Pitt, despite his hatred for the Great Commoner, because of his keen anxiety about his application. "I find," he wrote Bute, that

49. Lady Mary Coke to Bute, [25 July 1759], Bute Corresp.
50. Newcastle, "Memds. for the K.," 23 July 1759, 26 July 1759, 27 July 1759, B.M. Add. MS. 32,893, ff. 227, 283, 304, 306, 316.
51. An opinion shared by some later historians—see Sedgwick, *Letters from George III*, p. 26.
52. Bute to Pitt, 26 July 1759 [misdated 25 July], B.M. Add. MS. 36,797, f. 44 (copy); also published in *Chatham Correspondence*, I, 169–70, where it is misdated 15 July 1756 and thoroughly garbled.

the longer the thing is delay'd the more my eagerness for its success is encreas'd. The K[ing] and those he has consulted have treated [me] with less regard than they would have dar'd to have done any Member of Parliament; I hope you will agree with me in thinking that if this just request is refused that for my own honour, dignity, and character, I may keep no measures with these counsellors who have not prevented the K[ing] treating me with such unheard of contempt . . .[53]

Pitt thought he was being offered an opportunity to reingratiate himself at Leicester House, and he promptly replied that he applauded the prince's conduct and would do his best to forward Bute's wishes.[54] That same afternoon, when he met with his colleagues to draft a reply to the prince, Pitt "talk'd very strongly" and said that "He thought that the Prince would have been inexcusable, If He had not made such a Dutiful Tender of His Service: And that He, Mr. Pitt, would, in all places, avow His Opinion against it, if a Refusal was given."[55]

There is no question of Pitt's desire to oblige Bute, but unfortunately he was not at all clear as to just what the prince wanted. The answer to the request must not be negative, of that Pitt was sure, but as the application itself was general, he saw no reason why the answer need be specific. If the prince wanted a more definite statement, Pitt told Newcastle, he could always ask for a clarification. Much of the draft reply that was approved by George II was written by Pitt, and he assumed complete responsibility for the entire letter, presumably hoping for credit with both the king and his grandson. New-

---

53. Prince of Wales to Bute, past seven [26 July 1759], Sedgwick, *Letters from George III*, p. 26.
54. Pitt to Bute, 27 July 1759, B.M. Add. MS. 36,796, f. 38.
55. Newcastle to Hardwicke, Friday near 4 o'clock [27 July 1759], B.M. Add. MS. 32,893, ff. 318–19.

castle was glad to have someone else shoulder the blame. "I think upon the whole," he wrote Hardwicke, "we are got off well."⁵⁶

On July 28th the king's answer was carried to Kew by one of His Majesty's Grooms.⁵⁷ The note itself was very brief, and highly uncommittal:

> I received your letter which is a mark of duty to me and have the highest satisfaction in your spirit & zeal for the defence of my Kingdoms. It is my intention to give you on a proper occasion an opportunity of exerting them.⁵⁸

Officially, Leicester House was satisfied. Bute wrote Lord Huntingdon, the Prince's Master of the Horse, that he and the prince were happy that "His Majesty has been pleased to approve of so noble a petition."⁵⁹ In private, Bute and the prince were incensed. As soon as George received the king's reply he wrote Bute: "You will see by H.M. letter how shuffling it is and unworthy of a British Monarch; the conduct of this old K. makes me asham'd of being his grandson; he treats me in the same manner, his knave and councellor the D. of N. does all people, for this answer by some may be look'd upon as agreeing to my petition, by those who think further, as an absolute refusal."⁶⁰

Pitt came to Leicester House on Monday, July 30, thinking he had done well. This illusion must have been quickly shattered, for just past noon the prince wrote Bute that he was "not much surpriz'd at this insolence of Pitt's" toward Bute, since

---

56. *Ibid.*
57. Newcastle to Andrew Stone, 1 August 1759, B.M. Add. MS. 32,893, ff. 407–8.
58. "Drat. His Majesty to the Prince of Wales July 27th 1759," B.M. Egerton MS. 3425, f. 68; also B.M. Add. MS. 32,893, f. 316.
59. Bute to [the Earl of Huntingdon], 31 July 1759, HMC, *Reginald Rawdon Hastings MSS* (1934), III, 137.
60. Prince of Wales to Bute, [28 July 1759], Sedgwick, *Letters from George III*, pp. 26–27.

"he has long shown a want of regard both of you my Dearest Friend and consequently of myself."[61]

That same afternoon the prince, "upon pins least my request should be refus'd," went to see the king.[62] Newcastle reported to Andrew Stone that "the P. of Wales came, & had an Audience of the King, . . . which lasted some *Seconds*. The King told me, the P. said, He came to thank His Majesty for His Promises. The King said, I will send to you—Or let you know, when the Occasion happens." This, to Newcastle, seemed a proper reply, and both he and the king again congratulated themselves that "We have got well off."[63]

If they thought that they had satisfied the prince and Bute they were completely mistaken. Bute had made it clear to Pitt on Monday morning that the king's answer of the 28th was insufficient, that something more had to be done, "And that immediately." What was proposed by Pitt was that the prince should tour the camps at Portsmouth and Chatham and review the regiments of Guards.[64] Prince George's own thoughts were more radical; he wondered if he might not serve as a volunteer.[65] Certainly the idea of reviewing the troops was an innocuous alternative, for the prince would have no military rank and would always be accompanied by the commander-in-chief, Lord Ligonier.

Even this moderate suggestion was too extreme for George II. When Newcastle, urged on by Pitt and Lady Yarmouth, finally worked up enough nerve to broach the matter to the king on August 3, he received at first "an Absolute Negative," and after a long discussion George II would agree only to

---

61. Prince of Wales to Bute, past 12 [30 July 1759], Sedgwick, *Letters from George III*, p. 27.
62. *Ibid.*
63. Newcastle to Andrew Stone, 1 August 1759, B.M. Add. MS. 32,893, f. 408.
64. *Ibid.*
65. Prince of Wales to Bute, past 12 [30 July 1759], Sedgwick, *Letters from George III*, p. 27.

postpone a final decision.[66] Pitt could do nothing but report to Bute on August 6th that "it is with most real concern that I acquaint Your Lordship that I have nothing satisfactory to impart on the very interesting subject you did me the honour to mention in our last conversation."[67] Despite Pitt's assurance that he would keep on trying, the reply he received from the earl was the strongest statement yet to come from Leicester House on the subject:

> I am extremely concerned to observe by your letter, that all endeavours have proved hitherto unsuccessful, in regard to a business the Prince has so much at heart; I need not tell you that He Complains bitterly of the extreme neglect He ever meets with, in any matter (be it what it will) that immediately concerns Himself: the most gentle patient dispositions may at last be so soured, that all the prudential reasons and arguments in the world will not prevent very bad effects, very pernicious consequences; nothing shall be wanting on my part to preserve peace and good humour; but at the same time I will not be answerable for the consequences of this treatment, . . . .[68]

The threat in Bute's letter was obvious but general; the king's obstinacy was a specific barrier. Pitt and Newcastle did want George II to agree to this "trifle," but they were not willing to push the king too far over what they considered a secondary matter. As a result, nothing was done, despite the

---

66. Newcastle to Andrew Stone, 4 August 1759, B.M. Add. MS. 32,893, f. 480; for the urging of Lady Yarmouth and Pitt see "Memds. for the K.," 31 July 1759, B.M. Add. MS. 32,893, f. 392; "Business with My Lord Hardwicke," 2 August 1759, B.M. Add. MS. 32,893, ff. 425–26; "Memds. for the K.," 2 August 1759, 3 August 1759, B.M. Add. MS. 32,893, ff. 431–32, 469–70.

67. Pitt to Bute, 6 August 1759, Bute MSS, quoted in Sedgwick, *Letters from George III*, p. 28.

68. Bute to Pitt, 7 August 1759, B.M. Add. MS. 36,797, ff. 44–45 (copy); pub. inaccurately in *Chatham Correspondence*, I, 416–17; pub. accurately in Namier, *England*, pp. 103–4.

agreement of virtually every important figure in the ministry that this was a minor affair where Leicester House might well be gratified at little cost.[69] Notations on the possibility of the prince's reviewing the troops appear with monotonous regularity in Newcastle's memoranda throughout August and September,[70] and he probably raised the matter on several occasions with George II, but no reply was made. The matter gradually faded into the background, as Bute and the prince became deeply involved in the troubles of Lord George Sackville and H. B. Legge, but the failure of the prince's request left yet another residue of hatred and mistrust at Leicester House.

---

69. Even the Duke of Devonshire, normally antagonistic to Leicester House, agreed that the request was a "trifle" and, "for the sake of Peace & quiet not to be hestitated upon": Devonshire to Newcastle, 24 August 1759, B.M. Add. MS. 32,894, ff. 434–35.

70. B.M. Add. MSS 32,894–96, *passim*.

SEVEN

# NEW FRUSTRATIONS

The quarrel with Pitt had undermined the foundation of the political alliance system built by Bute between 1755–1757. In the second half of 1759 the rest of the edifice crumbled as Bute and the prince were faced with the disgrace of their leading military adviser, Lord George Sackville, and the complete alienation of their last ministerial ally, H. B. Legge.

Sackville is best known for his role as secretary of state for the colonies during the American Revolution. In the 1750's, however, he was considered one of the most promising young English field officers. His favor at Leicester House had dropped sharply when he had deserted the expeditionary forces in the fall of 1758,[1] but he rose once more into the good graces of the Prince of Wales when he was given the command of all English forces in Germany.[2] Certainly cordial relations were fully restored by the summer of 1759, when Sackville went so far as to send Bute Prince Ferdinand's secret memorandum containing the army's campaign plan for the summer, a document he considered so confidential "as to make it improper for me to write to the Ministry upon."[3] Lord George's disagreement with his commander's ideas only served to increase Bute's esteem for him, since Ferdinand was strongly disliked at Leicester House, "from family Considerations."[4]

On August 1, the allied forces won a major victory over

1. Newcastle to Hardwicke, 5 October 1758, B.M. Add. MS. 32,884, f. 261; "C.V.," Newcastle House, 31 October 1758, B.M. Add. MS. 32,885, f. 154.
2. Bute to Sackville, 17 November 1758, HMC, *Stopford-Sackville MSS*, I, 54.
3. Sackville to Bute, 18 July 1759, Bute MSS.
4. Newcastle to Hardwicke, 22 September 1759, B.M. Add. MS. 32,896, f. 41.

the French at Minden, a victory marred only by the failure of the cavalry, under Sackville, to advance when so ordered. Lord George felt that Ferdinand's charge that he had disobeyed orders was motivated solely by political malice. Finding himself "too sensibly hurt" to trust his own judgment, Sackville placed his future completely in Bute's hands, even relying on his friend to decide whether or not he should resign from the army.[5] The earl faced a real problem. He and the prince had viewed Sackville as a "very useful man," as one of the "tools" they hoped to use in their political plans. But his usefulness was now much diminished, and Bute urged caution on the prince,[6] lest they be dragged down with the disgraced general.

Sackville returned to London on September 7 and quickly discovered the seriousness of his situation. The government was united against him, for to support him would be to question England's ally, Prince Ferdinand.[7] George II made his opinion clear by sending Ferdinand a large cash present and making him a Knight of the Garter.[8] Even Bute, who pleaded the death of Princess Elizabeth as an excuse, refused to see Sackville. Bute still represented Sackville's final hope, however, and he clung desperately to that hope, lamenting his "unhappy situation" in being unable to see the earl.[9]

Sackville soon decided that the only way to clear his name was to apply for a court martial. When he notified Pitt of this intention he received a very cold reply,[10] and on the next day, September 10, George II dismissed the general from the

5. Sackville to Bute, 3 August 1759, Bute MSS.
6. Prince of Wales to Bute, Nine [11 August 1759], Sedgwick, *Letters from George III*, pp. 29–30.
7. Sackville to Bute, 9 September 1759, HMC, *Stopford-Sackville MSS*, I, 315.
8. Pitt to Bute, Wednesday morning [15 August 1759], Bute Corresp.
9. Sackville to Bute, 9 September 1759, HMC, *Stopford-Sackville MSS*, I, 315.
10. Pitt to Sackville, 9 September 1759, Bute Corresp. (copy).

## NEW FRUSTRATIONS

army.[11] Bute sympathized, but made it clear that he could not intervene with the ministers on Lord George's behalf.[12]

Bute was careful not to cut off Sackville completely; a son of the Duke of Dorset might someday prove valuable. When the Common Council of London considered inserting a clause derogatory to Lord George in an address to the king, Bute used his influence with one of the members, John Paterson, to block the move.[13] Aside from this one action, Bute did not take any positive steps on Sackville's behalf. The former general, however, continued to inform Bute of every nuance in his battle with the ministry.[14] The earl's brief replies contrasted sharply with Lord George's long and detailed reports.[15]

The ministry finally agreed to the court martial in January, and the trial took place in March and early April. No one but Sackville could have been surprised when he was found guilty, and the king and Newcastle were disappointed only by the judges' failure to impose the death sentence.

The court martial over, Lord George began his rehabilitation. However he may have acted at Minden, he demonstrated ample courage in his drive to reestablish himself in English society. When most men expected him to retire to his family estates in disgrace, he appeared instead in the House of Commons. Bute had restrained Sackville from calling at either Leicester or Savile House since his return to England, but now Lord George was determined that Bute and the prince should publicly demonstrate their oft-asserted friendship.

On April 17th Sir Harry Erskine warned Bute that Sackville intended to wait on the Prince of Wales in one week.

11. Sackville to Bute, 10 September 1759, B.M. Add. MS. 36,796, f. 42.
12. Bute to Sackville, 9 September 1759, B.M. Add. MS. 36,796, f. 41.
13. Paterson to Bute, 14 September 1759, Bute MSS.
14. Sackville to Bute, 9 November 1759, 3 December 1759, B.M. Add. MS. 36,796, ff. 43–44.
15. E.g. Sackville to Bute, 17 January 1760 (misdated 1759), Bute MSS; Bute to Sackville, [18 January 1760] (misdated 1759), HMC, *Stopford-Sackville MSS*, I, 314.

Erskine had tried to dissuade him, but Lord George insisted that if Bute and the Prince would not receive him he "must skulk about in the country as an undone man," and would "look upon it as abandoning him for ever."[16] Rumors connecting Sackville with Leicester House were already common, and Bute quickly intervened through Erskine to prevent what must have proven a very embarrassing audience. Realizing that he had no alternative, Sackville not only gave in, but thanked Bute for the "honour" of his "protection."[17]

Lady Yarmouth had told Newcastle that the prince might receive Lord George,[18] and the duke immediately relayed the news to Hardwicke. The lawyer wisely replied that it was best for the king to take no notice of it, for "if the King was either *directly or indirectly* to send any Intimation against it, 'twill be called Persecution."[19] George II would have done well to follow Hardwicke's advice. Instead, on April 23, the day after Sackville had agreed not to appear at Savile House, the king notified Bute and the Princess of Wales that he had "forbid Lord George Sackville the Court."[20] The obvious implication was that the prince should do the same.

George II's message infuriated the prince, who saw it as interference in his personal affairs and also as the final step in the persecution of an innocent man.[21] Yet another wedge was driven between Leicester House and the government, as Bute

16. Erskine to Bute, 27 April 1760, Bute Corresp.
17. Lord Talbot to Bute, Wednesday Evening [22 April 1760], Bute Corresp.; Erskine to Bute, 22 April 1760, Bute Corresp.
18. Lady Yarmouth to Newcastle, [18 April 1760], B.M. Add. MS. 32,904, f. 430. Torrens's misreading of Lady Yarmouth's French (Torrens, *Cabinets*, II, 541) has led other authors to state that Sackville *was* received at Leicester House: e.g. Alan Valentine, *Lord George Germain* (Oxford, 1962), p. 75.
19. Hardwicke to Newcastle, 20 April 1760, B.M. Add. MS. 32,904, f. 455.
20. Duke of Devonshire to Bute, 23 April 1760, Bute Corresp.; Walpole, *George II*, III, 273-74; Mr Rigby to the Duke of Bedford, 29 April 1760, *Bedford Corresp.*, II, 414.
21. Prince of Wales to Bute, [23 April 1760], Sedgwick, *Letters from George III*, p. 43.

and the prince blamed not only the king, but Newcastle and Pitt as well, for the downfall of their friend.[22]

Despite the added friction between the junior court and the administration, however, Leicester House emerged from the fall of Lord George relatively unscathed. The rumor that the prince favored Sackville had spread in spite of Bute's care to avoid public demonstrations of sympathy. His caution in dealing with Lord George himself, however, did have the beneficial result of minimizing the stigma attached to the heir. And Bute was successful in his handling of Sackville himself. Although he had really done very little for the unfortunate officer, Bute managed to convince Sackville that he had accomplished everything in his power.[23] When Sackville passed through London in August he thanked Bute for "the very real acts of friendship shown me by your Lordship when I had the greatest occasion for Countenance and Protection."[24]

Meanwhile the death of Heneage Legge on August 30, 1759, had begun a sequence of events which were to lead to the loss of Bute's last important parliamentary ally. By his brother's death, H. B. Legge, the chancellor of the Exchequer, succeeded to the position of surveyor of the petty customs in the Port of London. This office was covered by the Place Acts and, since it devolved directly to Legge, the chancellor's seat in the Commons was automatically vacated. Newcastle feared that Legge would retain the highly profitable position and insist on a long deferred peerage as well, thus leaving both the House of Commons and the Chancellorship. The longer Legge remained in Hampshire, however, the less country life appealed to him, and by early October he had reached a compromise settlement with the duke.[25]

22. [Bute to Lord Talbot], 23 April 1760, Bute Corresp. (draft); "C.V.," Newcastle House, 2 October 1759, B.M. Add. MS. 32,896, f. 223; Newcastle, "Secret Memds.," 5 October 1759, B.M. Add. MS. 32,896, ff. 302-3.
23. Erskine to Bute, 15 May 1760, Bute MSS.
24. Sackville to Bute, 8 August 1760, Bute MSS.
25. Legge to Bute, 27 September 1759, Bute Corresp.

Once Legge had decided to remain as chancellor the problem of his reelection arose. The Marquis of Winchester had just succeeded his father as Duke of Bolton, thus vacating his seat for Hampshire in the House of Commons. A group of Legge's friends asked him to stand for this seat, instead of returning to his safe constituency at Orford. Legge reluctantly agreed, apparently on the assumption that his election would be uncontested.

Bute also had an interest in the electoral affairs of Hampshire. A Leicester House adherent, Lord Carnarvon, eldest son of the Duke of Chandos and member of Parliament for Winchester, had lost control of that borough to the Powlett (Bolton) family in 1758.[26] Carnarvon and Bute had immediately begun to lay plans to destroy the Duke of Bolton's "interest" in both the borough of Winchester and the county of Hampshire in the general election of 1761.[27] By the time the Duke of Bolton died, Carnarvon and his friends were ready with the nomination of Simeon Stuart, the son of a local baronet, for the Hampshire vacancy.[28]

Both parties saw the election as having implications far beyond a simple choice between two candidates. Lord Clanricarde reminded Newcastle that the Whigs had only recently wrested control of Hampshire away from the Tories, and added that whoever won this contest would "settle their party for life." When Newcastle read that "such my Lord is the present doctrine of politicks that whiges are no longer whiges," and heard that Stuart was supported by "many who called themselves Whigs," he recognized the influence of the pernicious idea that there was no longer any difference between the political parties.[29] Confident that he still knew who was a Whig,

26. Hans Stanley to Newcastle, 24 November 1759, B.M. Add. MS. 32,899, ff. 83–84.
27. Carnarvon to Bute, 26 August, 1759, Bute MSS.
28. On Stuart see McKelvey, "Bute and George III," pp. 231–32.
29. Clanricarde to Newcastle, 3 November 1759, 13 November 1759, 1 Novem-

## NEW FRUSTRATIONS

Newcastle hastened to assure the Duke of Bolton that Legge would receive all his support.[30]

Stuart gave every indication of making a real attempt for the seat. The first public subscription in Hampshire history was raised to support his candidacy. Stuart himself told Bute that his followers "seemed determined to stand a Poll," and Newcastle heard the same report from his friends in the county.[31] Legge and the duke were convinced that "Mr. Stuart will run us hard."[32]

Simeon Stuart could never have caused so much concern without influential backing. Newcastle and his associates knew that the "Tory" candidate had support in London. As early as November 4, John Page wrote Newcastle that "Mr. Stewarts Interest seems to receive a considerable Addition of Strength from Letters wrote by Ld. Bute in his favour."[33] On that same day Edmund Bramston wrote Bute that he had received the earl's letter, "and in consequence of it appeared for Mr. Stuart at the late Nomination," although he would normally have supported Bolton's nominee.[34] Bramston was one of the Gentlemen Ushers of the Privy Chamber to the princess dowager; if he valued his £300 salary he could scarcely disregard Bute's instructions.

Despite Bolton's great influence in Hampshire, the duke was sufficiently unpopular that Stuart might have won the election[35] had it not been for the tremendous pressure which the government could bring to bear in that county. The large

---

ber 1759, Legge to Newcastle, 2 November 1759, B.M. Add. MS. 32,898, ff. 73, 235, 24, 55.
30. Newcastle to Bolton, 4 November 1759, B.M. Add. MS. 32,898, f. 90.
31. Simeon Stuart to Bute, 12 November 1759, Bute MSS; Clanricarde to Newcastle, 3 November 1759, B.M. Add. MS. 32,898, f. 73.
32. Legge to Newcastle, 2 November 1759, B.M. Add. MS. 32,898, f. 55.
33. John Page to Newcastle, 4 November 1759, B.M. Add. MS. 32,898, f. 92.
34. Edmund Bramston to Bute, 4 November 1759, Bute MSS.
35. W. Battine to Revd. Mr. Handis, 20 November 1759, B.M. Add. MS. 32,898, ff. 409–10.

dockyards and military camps in Hampshire employed or supported hundreds of voters. As W. Battine pointed out, Bolton's influence had always carried Hampshire so long as the ministry had backed him.[36]

Bute was aware of this problem, and tried to curb official support of Legge. He assigned to Gilbert Elliot, as one of the lords of the Admiralty, the task of restraining Newcastle in that department. Elliot claimed some success, but he was unable to prevent official letters in support of Legge from being written both to the docks at Portsmouth and to the Depot of the Sick and Wounded Seamen.[37] Simeon Stuart estimated that the first letter, to the commissioner of the Dock, had ensured some four hundred votes for the chancellor.[38]

By November 24 both sides had completed canvasses, and it was clear that Stuart had no hope of winning the election.[39] Anxious to avoid further expense, each party having already spent some £5000,[40] Stuart and his supporters capitulated.[41] Legge immediately thanked Newcastle for the "Zeal" he had shown on his behalf and Newcastle, in turn, assured the successful candidate that "I am very Happy if I have been of any Service to You in Your Election—My Endeavours, & My Declarations were not wanting."[42] Hans Stanley, one of Newcastle's friends, rejoiced that "this essay of a Scotch ministerial intervention in an English County so considerable and so well affected having received so due and so thorough a chastisement,

---

36. *Ibid.*
37. Gilbert Elliot to Bute, 4 o'clock [13 November 1759], Bute MSS.
38. Simeon Stuart to Bute, 15 November 1759, Bute MSS.
39. Hans Stanley to Newcastle, 24 November 1759, B.M. Add. MS. 32,899, ff. 83–84; Stuart to Bute, 25 November 1759, Bute MSS.
40. Legge to Samuel Martin, 5 December 1759, in [John Butler],*Some Account of the Character of the Late Right Honourable Henry Bilson Legge* (London, 1764), p. 15.
41. Stanley to Newcastle, 24 November 1759, B.M. Add. MS. 32,899, ff. 83–84.
42. Legge to Newcastle, 24 November 1759, Newcastle to Legge, 27 November 1759, B.M. Add. MS. 32,899, ff. 77, 146.

will stop pretensions at the generall Elections."[43] Newcastle happily agreed that "the Example will do good."[44]

Neither Stuart nor Bute, however, had given up their "pretensions" for the general election of 1761. In the same letter in which he notified Bute of his concession, Stuart said that he and his friends thought it best to await the next election "before we discover our strength."[45]

Legge had won the election but lost his tie with Leicester House. Although he had not intentionally joined battle with the prince, the result was equally disastrous. Bute had supported Stuart before he knew that Legge was to be a candidate,[46] and Legge knew of neither Stuart's candidacy nor Bute's intervention until he was committed to stand for the seat.[47] It is illustrative of the lack of communication between the Leicester House leaders and their parliamentary allies that Bute and Legge were ignorant of each other's plans, but the fact remains that neither party had any intention of embarrassing the other when they entered the contest.

Bute still hoped to salvage something from his defeat. On November 25, the day after Stuart conceded, the earl sent for Samuel Martin, Legge's closest political associate. As Martin reported the conversation to Legge, Bute told him that "having an Opportunity of saving you, he had embraced it," and convinced Stuart to concede.[48] Actually, Stuart had conceded solely on the basis of his canvass and without consulting Bute, but the latter did not intend to let this interfere with his plans

43. Stanley to Newcastle, 24 November 1759, B.M. Add. MS. 32,899, ff. 83–84.
44. Newcastle to Stanley, 27 November 1759, B.M. Add. MS. 32,899, f. 148.
45. I.e. go to a poll. Stuart to Bute, 25 November 1759, Bute MSS.
46. Apparently Bute first heard of Legge's candidacy in a letter from Carnarvon dated November 3: B.M. Add. MS. 36,796, f. 43.
47. Legge to Newcastle, 2 November 1759, B.M. Add. MS. 32,898, f. 73.
48. Samuel Martin to Legge, 25 November 1759, in [Butler], *Legge*, p. 14. Only one of the letters published in this pamphlet has been discovered in MS, but that so closely adheres to the published version that it seems safe to regard the others as accurate too.

for Legge. Bute was willing to be magnanimous, Martin wrote:

> Lord B. added, that neither he, nor the greater Person, whose Name hath been used during the Competition, would ever treat you with the more Coldness for what hath happened: your path having been taken under an Ignorance of their Views and Intentions; that Lord B. expected however, as he had a Claim upon you, in right of Friendship, that you will concur with Him, and give your Aid to the Person he shall recommend, at a future Election.[49]

Legge did not answer this message for ten days, and in the interim he implied to Simeon Stuart that he wished that the two of them might be successful candidates for Hampshire at that election.[50] He repeated the same thought, though more cautiously, in his reply to Martin on December 5, when he said that he would gladly support Stuart if the Whigs and Dissenters of Hampshire approved.[51] This was far from sufficient. Angered at what he considered Legge's evasiveness, Bute ordered Martin on December 12th to tell the chancellor that "he should bid adieu to the County of Southampton at the general Election, and assist, as far as lay in his power, the P——— of W———'s Nomination of two Members."[52]

Legge replied that he was "determined to submit to any Consequence rather than incur so great a Disgrace" as to desert his Whig allies. Bute could not see how the dissenters of Hampshire could prevail over the Prince of Wales. He warned Legge that unless he cooperated fully, the prince's "Prejudices" against him could not be curbed.[53]

The unfortunate chancellor made one last attempt to sal-

49. *Ibid.*
50. Simeon Stuart to Bute, 27 November 1759, Bute MSS.
51. Legge to Martin, 5 December 1759, in [Butler], *Legge*, p. 16.
52. Legge's transcription of Martin's remarks, quoted in [Butler], *Legge*, p. 16.
53. *Ibid.*, p. 17.

vage something from the wreckage of his past favor. His final letter to Bute concludes:

> God forbid Mr. L. should be suspected of triumphing over the Prince of Wales's Inclinations. . . . Surely his Lordsp. cannot doubt but Mr. L. should be extreamly happy if he could find himself in a Situation where he might have the honour of obeying the Prince of Wales's commands & seconding his wishes without breaking the faith He has openly & publickly pledged to the County of Southampton.[54]

His appeal was totally unsuccessful. When Prince George read Legge's letter, he wrote Bute a note which not only marked the end of Legge's connection with Leicester House but also indicated the direction in which the heir and his favorite were moving. "L[egge's] letter," the Prince wrote, "makes me more incens'd against him than ever; it is drawn up in his usual tricking manner; my Dearest Friend we must look out for new tools our old one's having all deserted us; if I am but steady and have your assistance, we may make them all smart for their ingratitude."[55]

The break between Bute and Legge completed the destruction of the alliance built up in 1755 between Leicester House and the opposition. This did not mean, however, that Bute had lost all influence in the cabinet. Newcastle, despite the obvious lack of return for his efforts, was still willing to undertake small tasks for the Prince of Wales, and Lord Holdernesse, the secretary of state for the Northern Department, had for some time been trying to ingratiate himself with Bute. When Bute had criticized Pitt in 1758 for the sparseness of the information he was sending the Prince, the earl had pointed

54. [Legge to Bute, December 1759], Bute MSS; also pub. in [Butler], *Legge*, pp. 17–18.
55. Prince of Wales to Bute, Past Seven [23 December 1759], Sedgwick, *Letters from George III*, pp. 34–35.

out that the other secretary's reports were both fuller and more punctual. Holdernesse knew how much this pleased Bute, and he provided the heir with detailed accounts of all government business.[56]

This sort of attention could scarcely be kept secret. By the fall of 1759 it had become a scandal. Holdernesse was not only sending Bute the information coming into his department, but was also forwarding all the news he could glean from his colleagues' offices.[57] Newcastle reported jealously to Hardwicke that, as a result of all this attention, "Holdernesse is the Great Favourite" with Bute.[58] Hardwicke replied that, while "what is said of Lord H. is very extraordinary; . . . I cannot persuade my self that his Favour at L. House has any thing solid in it. It arises from little fiddle faddle Attentions & Communications to Lord B., with which he is flattered for the time."[59] Hardwicke was right; Holdernesse's favor with Bute did not have a solid base. Just as when Legge replaced Pitt as the prince's favorite politician, it was clear that this was a case of making do with second best, that "They don't equally esteem Him."[60]

Hardwicke was wrong, however, in describing Holdernesse's reports to Bute as "fiddle faddle." Bute, for example, was probably better informed than anyone outside the cabinet on the negotiations between England and Spain in 1759 and 1760. Virtually all of the important documents concerning this affair were sent to Bute by Holdernesse, although they were under the jurisdiction of Pitt's department.[61] And when Newcastle attempted to open a very delicate peace negotiation with France, through Joseph Yorke, English minister to the

---

56. E.g. Holdernesse to Bute, 24 March 1759, Bute MSS.
57. "C.V.," Newcastle House, 2 October 1759, B.M. Add. MS. 32,896, f. 224.
58. Newcastle, "Secret Memds.," 5 October 1759, B.M. Add. MS. 32,896, f. 303.
59. Hardwicke to Newcastle, 6 October 1759, B.M. Add. MS. 32,896, f. 324.
60. "C.V.," Newcastle House, 2 October 1759, B.M. Add. MS. 32,896, f. 223.
61. Bute MSS. 14 December 1759–26 September 1760, *passim*.

Netherlands, he found that Bute not only knew of the opening, but was actually better informed than Newcastle himself —and this in a matter which the duke was trying to keep secret from Pitt!⁶²

Holdernesse never really received much benefit from all of this attention to Bute. Certainly he never attained the high position at Leicester House which Newcastle and Pitt thought he had. Pitt said that Holdernesse was in such good repute with the Prince of Wales that he would be the "vortex" of "the next Reign."⁶³ And Newcastle agreed with Viry that "if the Prince of Wales should come to the Crown, ... there is no one Minister so sure of being kept, & in Credit" as Holdernesse.⁶⁴ Hardwicke's earlier opinion, that the secretary's "Favour at L. House" had nothing "solid in it," was much more nearly accurate. Holdernesse was useful for the moment, but, once George III ascended the throne, he was the first minister to be forced out of office.

Even while he relied on Holdernesse, Bute never gave up his dream that Pitt and the Grenvilles would return, properly contrite, to the bosom of Leicester House. In the fall of 1759, when Lord Temple renewed his request to the king for the Garter, it seemed for a while as if that time had come.⁶⁵ When George II refused to give such a dignity to a man he hated, Temple forced the issue by resigning as Lord Privy Seal on the opening day of Parliament.⁶⁶

The prospect of a falling out between Pitt and Temple, on the one side, and George II and Newcastle, on the other, was highly pleasing to Bute. The very stability of the ministry over

62. "C.V.," Newcastle House, 30 October 1759, B.M. Add. MS. 32,897, ff. 498–99.
63. Newcastle to Hardwicke, 2 January 1760, B.M. Add. MS. 32,901, f. 43.
64. "C.V.," Newcastle House, 21 November 1759, B.M. Add. MS. 32,899, ff. 11–12.
65. For a full relation of this sordid business, see Lewis M. Wiggin, *The Faction of Cousins* (New Haven, 1958), pp. 219–23.
66. Temple to Bute, Wednesday morning [14 November 1759], Bute Corresp.

the past year and a half had been one of the most important factors in decreasing the influence of Bute and the prince. If this solid façade could be broken, then the search for powerful allies would begin anew and the influence of Leicester House would be vastly increased. But this blissful prospect lasted only two days, for then the king capitulated and gave Temple the Garter.[67] Viry, who saw Bute after Temple's reconciliation with George II, reported that although Leicester House "were very well pleased with My Lord Temple for quitting, . . . they were quite otherwise, upon his coming in again."[68]

Temple himself was unimportant; his significance rested solely on his relationship to Pitt. Bute was never able to reconcile himself to the loss of the Great Commoner. Even Pitt's failure to accomplish the prince's wishes in the army request and his hostility to Lord George Sackville could not convince Bute that Leicester House was better off without him.

By 1759 Pitt considered his connection with Leicester House as a purely formal one.[69] When the problem of poor communication between the secretary and the prince arose again in late 1759, Pitt adopted a high moral tone. He protested that "His condition was very hard indeed," for

> Nobody wishes more than I do, That the King would order his Servants to communicate His Business to the Prince of Wales; And even to order His Royal Highness to assist us at Council: But, since that was not the King's Pleasure, He did not think it was right for Any of the King's Servants to inform His Royal Highness of the King's Business. That What made it very hard upon Him (Mr. Pitt) was, that My Lord Holdernesse communicated

67. Temple to Bute, 16 November 1759, Bute Corresp.
68. "C.V.," Newcastle House, 22 November 1759, B.M. Add. MS. 32,899, f. 33.
69. "C.V.," Newcastle House, 28 November 1759, B.M. Add. MS. 32,899, ff. 164-65.

Every thing to the Prince of Wales. That *that* had made Him (Mr. Pitt) very Ill there, & would make Him worse Every Day.[70]

Newcastle considered this a remarkable statement, and Pitt's moral stance should not be taken too seriously.[71] The secretary had demonstrated his eagerness to appease the prince in the matter of the army, and he still made occasional attempts to give Bute the thorough information on governmental affairs which the earl desired.[72] When all of his efforts failed to ingratiate him, however, Pitt took refuge in the idea that he was in fact pursuing the moral course and was being undermined at Leicester House by the unethical behavior of his colleague.

In December, 1759, Bute sent Pitt the friendliest letter he had written the secretary in more than a year, complimenting him on the brilliant successes of the year, and adding that "Lord Bute is not a little pleased to think how much this immense success is owing to Mr. Pitt's ardour, Steadiness, and ability."[73] Bute may already have been contemplating yet another attempt at reconciliation, for such a move was made in the spring.

Toward the end of April, 1760, Bute proposed to Gilbert Elliot that he should tell Pitt of "the personal regard I have ever had for him, unshaken by the long chain of unfortunate circumstances, that have gradually brought on the distance now subsisting."[74] Elliot repeated Bute's remarks to Pitt and then told Bute of the secretary's generally favorable response.

70. "C.V.," Newcastle House, 10 November 1759, B.M. Add. MS. 32,898, ff. 204–5.
71. *Ibid.*
72. For an excellent example, see Pitt to Bute, Saturday morning [April, 1759], Bute MSS.
73. Bute to Pitt, [December 1759], *Chatham Correspondence*, I, 475.
74. Bute to Elliot, 30 April 1760, Minto MSS, National Library of Scotland; pub. in Namier, *England*, pp. 104–5 (somewhat inaccurately).

Elliot's report convinced the earl that Pitt misunderstood "my character, my views, my way of thinking." In hopes, therefore, of reestablishing their former "fraternal union" Bute empowered Elliot to contact Pitt again, "& if you please, you may tell him, that on the strictest search I can discover no one idea in my mind, that opposes drawing the knot of union as tight as ever." Bute, "feeling in my own breast the generous publick principle I act on," left it to Elliot's discretion whether or not Pitt's response would justify a meeting between the two principals, where their differences might be "bury'd in oblivion."[75]

Pitt could scarcely be expected to appreciate the role of a prodigal client, now to be received back by his forgiving masters. When Elliot broached Bute's ideas to the secretary, all of the latter's long suppressed anger burst forth.[76]

"Favour [is] not every thing in this Country," Pitt said, and "the singleing all confidence into one hand to the exclusion of all mankind," together with "the flippant use of the P[rince's] name gives disgust." Bute "has all confidence, all habitude, gives hourly indications of an imperious nature." Pitt thought Bute's accusations most unfair. Should he be criticized for gaining the favor of Lady Yarmouth? Had Bute forgotten how Pitt and Leicester House came together in 1755, when the favorite pleaded his own disadvantages and inadequacy, and made it clear to Pitt and his friends "that all would be in our hands in a future day?" But then, "after some interval told shortly, that he himself was destined for the Treasury" and "that he agreed to it mostly on my account, as every other person in that situation would sap and undermine me."

75. *Ibid.*
76. The following quotations are all from this document: Elliot's memorandum, [early May 1760], Minto MSS, National Library of Scotland; pub. in slightly different form, in Namier, *England*, pp. 105–7.

Pitt felt that he had carried out his part of the bargain:

> As to want of confidence & communication so much complained of: I have acted upon the concerted plan, I have effectually barrd the entrance to those who were meant to be excluded, carryed on the war on its plan, armed the Country even Scotland . . . but I have not carefully transmitted every little scrap of paper, all the little paultry detail, I have not waited for direction & approbation, but seized the moment when I coud to secure these measures.

"In such circumstances," Pitt found it hard "to be continually meeting obstruction instead of support from Leicester House." "Now every one [was] more at home at Leicester House than I, . . . persons talked of to day as the lowest and most unable men to morrow caressd & confidentially used." Bute was unreasonable to expect such close cooperation from Pitt: "I will not be rid with a check rein, . . . I cant bear a touch of command." Such being the case, Pitt concluded, "I know it is impossible for me to act in a responsible ministerial office with L[ord] B[ute]." At the same time, "my age infirmitys turn of mind make it impossible for me to undertake new oppositions, . . . neither will I retire peevish and discontented but recur to the P[rince] and Lord B[ute's] friendships to put me in some honourable bystanding office where I have no responsibility but aid counsels if calld upon. Let me conclude with saying, by distrusting his friends he'll become dependent on his enemys. I will even make way for his greatness, assist it only I cannot make part of it."[77]

Following this debacle it is not surprising that Pitt and Bute "were very ill together."[78] Nonetheless, convinced that Pitt was the one politician whose cooperation was essential

---

77. For Count Viry's somewhat different version of this transaction, see B.M. Add. MS. 32,909, ff. 343–45.
78. *Ibid.*, f. 343.

for a smooth transfer of power to George III and his favorite, Bute still felt a hearty "respect" for the Great Commoner.[79] Pitt's rebuff, had it come from any other man, would have insured Bute's life-long hatred, but the earl valued Pitt so highly that by the fall of 1760 he was planning yet another attempt to contact him.[80] Ironically, the secretary was thinking along the same lines. Well aware that he was "ill at Leicester" and worried by the rumor that Bute would support the Duke of Cumberland for commander-in-chief if Ligonier should die, Pitt told Lady Yarmouth on October 18, 1760, that he would "soon" go to Leicester House "to try His Fate."[81] But exactly one week later George II died. Neither side had made a move toward reconciliation while it still would have been meaningful.

79. Newcastle, "In the greatest Secrecy," 18 July 1760, B.M. Add. MS. 32,908, f. 343; Newcastle, "Secret Memds.," 25 July 1760, B.M. Add. MS. 32,909, f. 47.
80. "C.V.," Newcastle House, 8 August 1760, B.M. Add. MS. 32,909, f. 344.
81. Newcastle to Hardwicke, 18 October 1760, B.M. Add. MS. 32,913, f. 188.

EIGHT

## A NEW DIRECTION AT LEICESTER HOUSE?

The abortive negotiations with Pitt in the spring of 1760 confirmed the failure of the policy followed at Leicester House since 1755. At that time Princess Augusta and Lord Bute had sought security and influence by forming alliances with prominent politicians. Until 1757 all went well. Pitt, Legge, and the Grenvilles allied themselves with Leicester House; the Prince of Wales was permitted to remain with his mother; Bute became Groom of the Stole; and the Pittites forced their way into George II's government. Despite these victories, however, real success eluded the princess and her favorite. The new ministers found it impossible to serve both king and heir, and all of their ties with Leicester House were soon broken. By late 1759 the young court appeared to have even less influence than it had possessed four years earlier.

What was to be done? Perhaps the wisest course would have been to do nothing, to simply have awaited the death of the seventy-six-year-old king. But the prince and Bute, convinced that Britain was in mortal danger and could be saved only by their wisdom and courage, felt compelled to act. So long as the Pitt-Newcastle ministry remained united and victorious, however, any opposition designed to overthrow the administration must fail. The alternative was a holding action, an opposition of "noble simplicity," like that which Bubb Dodington had urged on Prince Frederick in 1749. Such an opposition, by occasionally challenging the ministry, and by emphasizing the "public good, and the public good only," would "fix the attention of mankind" on the heir and prepare both prince and subjects for a new reign.[1] Furthermore, this type of opposition, since it involved no hope of capturing the government, required no great politicians. Men like Pitt and Legge had proven themselves unreliable; though they might find Leicester House support useful, they could often do without it. Lesser men could be tied to the prince by stronger bonds.

There is no proof that Bute and the prince had decided on precisely this plan, but it is clear that they were convinced of the necessity, as the prince put it, of drawing "men to follow my banner."[2] They were trying to build a purely Leicester House faction with Bute as its sole leader. Their motive may have been nothing more than a desire to remind the world that the Prince of Wales had resources of his own. In any case, the key to such a strategy was enlarging the heir's support in Parliament. Members loyal to Leicester House could be used as spokesmen for the prince's ideas, or they might, at some future date, form the nucleus for a direct attack on the administration. In either instance, the larger the group, the more effective it would be. By early 1760 Bute could normally count on the support of ten M.P.s.[3] The general election of 1761 offered the best hope for increasing this faction, and Bute began planning for that event at least as early as 1759.

All elections in the eighteenth century were basically local contests, decided by the preponderance of "interest" in the individual counties and boroughs. Influential contacts in the

    1. Dodington, *Diary*, pp. 435ff.
    2. Prince of Wales to Bute, [circa 23 April 1760], Sedgwick, *Letters from George III*, p. 43.
    3. The occasion never arose for these men specifically to identify themselves, but the following M.P.s can be considered loyal to Bute: Gilbert Elliot, Sir Harry Erskine, Sir William Irby, John Ross Mackye, James Stuart Mackenzie, William Mure, Lord Carnarvon, John Gordon, Lord Pulteney, and Samuel Martin.

constituencies were, therefore, essential. Among the men who had attached themselves to the prince's Groom of the Stole were many who either possessed seats in Parliament or were able to influence elections. It was on this foundation that Bute intended to build for 1761.

Bute inherited little support from the Leicester House of Prince Frederick. Most of the late prince's adherents had formed new connections after his widow turned away from politics, and those who had remained in Augusta's favor—Egmont, Lee and Cresset—had quit in disgust when Bute gained complete ascendance at Leicester House. Some of the princess's lesser servants, however, were now at Bute's disposal. Sir Edmond Thomas, Augusta's treasurer, had given up his seat in the Commons in 1754, but he planned to stand for Glamorganshire in 1761. Sir William Irby, her chamberlain, held a secure seat for Bodmin. Also, now that Leicester House was again active politically, some of Frederick's friends wanted to renew their allegiance. The Duke of Chandos, for example, sought a place in Prince George's establishment and, although he was unsuccessful, was gratified to see his son, Lord Carnarvon, playing a key role in Bute's political maneuvers.[4] Lord Talbot, who was both an old associate of Prince Frederick's and a close friend of Bute's, reaffirmed his alliance to the new prince in 1759.[5]

Talbot is an unfortunate example of the type of man Bute frequently preferred to have around him. Horace Walpole acknowledged that Talbot was "a Lord of good parts," but he added that while he "had some wit, and a little tincture of a disordered understanding," he was "better known as a boxer and man of pleasure, than in the light of a statesman."[6] Even allowing for Walpole's normal exaggeration, Talbot was not

4. Chandos to Bute, 31 December 1759, Bute MSS.
5. Talbot to Bute, 12 August 1759, Bute MSS; see McKelvey, "Bute and George III," pp. 261–62.
6. Walpole, *George II*, I, 120–21; Walpole, *George III*, I, 36.

the sort of man Bute should have relied on for political counsel.

Fortunately, Bute also had the help of more competent friends, most of them Scots who were uneasy under Argyll's domination of Scottish politics. Gilbert Elliot had been attached to the earl since 1755. Since he had also retained the friendship of William Pitt, Elliot had been the logical intermediary in the attempt to restore relations between Bute and Pitt in the spring of 1760. When that negotiation failed, Elliot settled firmly into the Leicester House sphere. He was an ambitious politician, but no mere sycophant. Deeply concerned by the "second class" status of Scotland, he urged several Scottish reforms, the most important being his proposal for a Lowland militia.[7]

Sir Harry Erskine's friendship with Bute had been sealed in 1756, when Erskine had lost his army commission for voting against the subsidy treaties. After this he became completely dependent on Bute.[8] Erskine had influential contacts in Scotland, particularly through his relations, the St. Clairs, and he was able to aid Bute considerably when the earl began contesting Scottish elections.

Another Scottish M.P., John Ross Mackye, was totally devoted to Bute. Regularly, each year, he wrote Bute from Scotland, asking whether the earl would like him to come south to attend Parliament and, if so, when.[9] Typical is the letter of December 10, 1757: "whatever reasons I may have for staying at home, yet most willingly I acknowledge myself bound to obey your Call."[10]

Many Scots whose families were tainted with Jacobitism looked to Bute for salvation. They felt that his attachment to the Hanoverian Prince of Wales must remove any suspicion of

---

7. Elliot, *Border Elliots*, pp. 359ff.
8. Erskine to Bute, 7 December 1758, Bute MSS.
9. Mackye to Bute, 10 December 1757, 20 October 1758, 9 November 1759, Bute MSS.
10. Mackye to Bute, 10 December 1757, Bute MSS.

## A NEW DIRECTION?

disloyalty from those identified with him. When Lord Chesterfield wanted to introduce his cousin, Lord Strathmore, into London society, he took him to Bute, explaining that Strathmore's political principles were "extremely different from those absurd ones which his family too long entertained." Strathmore, Chesterfield said, wanted to be known as "one intirely belonging" to Bute.[11]

Lord Home had no connection with Jacobitism, but he was opposed to the Argyll faction in Scotland.[12] Before he left England to become governor of Gibraltar, Home asked Bute to safeguard his interests, and particularly to prevent his enemies from undermining his political position in Berwickshire.[13] Home was one of the Sixteen Peers of Scotland and enjoyed considerable influence in the Lowlands.

Bute's family added strength to his faction. His brother, James Stuart Mackenzie, sat in Parliament for the Ayr Burghs, and his landed wealth gave him weight in several constituencies. Bute's brother-in-law, Sir Robert Menzies, was not active in politics, but he did control a number of votes in Ross-shire.[14] Mr. Wortley, Bute's father-in-law, had the nomination of one member for Bossiney.[15] The earl himself, as principal landowner of the Isle of Bute, controlled elections in Buteshire and the burgh of Rothesay. The agent in charge of Bute's estates, William Mure, represented Renfrewshire in the House of Commons and was a leader among the gentry of that county.[16]

Many of Bute's associates were recent converts. Lord Cathcart, a Scottish Representative Peer, joined the Leicester

11. Chesterfield to Bute, 6 April 1759, Bute MSS; Bute presented Strathmore at Savile House on 12 April: Bute to Newcastle, 11 April 1759, B.M. Add. MS. 32,890, f. 3; compare the situation of the Earl of Aboyne: Aboyne to Bute, 18 March, 8 April 1760, Bute Corresp.
12. Home to Bute, 29 January 1758, Bute MSS.
13. Home to Bute, 16 July 1758, Bute MSS.
14. Menzies to Bute, 28 August 1760, Bute Corresp.
15. Memo on Cornish Boroughs, B.M. Add. MS. 32,907, f. 461.
16. Mure was completely devoted to Bute in his politics: Mure to Bute, 24 November 1758, Bute MSS.

House group late in 1758. Cathcart's reputation was not good (Mackenzie called him a "meer time server"[17]) but he was an active politician and held considerable influence in Clackmannanshire.[18] Lord Aberdour switched from Argyll's faction because his father, Lord Morton, strongly disapproved of his marriage. Since Morton was a leader in the government party, this made Aberdour's application to Bute logical. Besides, as Hardwicke observed, even if there had been no elopement, "it is not to be wonder'd at that a Scotchman, & a young Man, should apply to the Quarter of Leicester" House.[19]

Political enmity was the cause of Lord Pulteney's conversion. His father, Lord Bath, was involved in a bitter struggle with Lord Powis in Shropshire. Powis was supported by Newcastle, and Leicester House became involved when Pulteney raised a regiment and obtained the Prince of Wales' blessing for it.[20] Though Pulteney was "a young man burdened with difficult parents, an unhappy youth, little character, and no merit,"[21] his father's enormous wealth made him a prize worth seeking.

Other men worked more directly as Bute's political agents. John Paterson, a member of the London Common Council, acted as the earl's representative in city affairs.[22] Samuel Martin, who had long been Legge's alter ego, deserted his master for Bute after the Hampshire by-election.[23] Bute seemed a more promising patron, and the earl, in turn, found Martin's political experience very useful.[24]

17. Mackenzie to Bute, 13 January 1759, Bute MSS.
18. Cathcart to Bute, 18 October 1759, Bute MSS.
19. Erskine to Bute, 23 August 1759, Bute MSS; Hardwicke to Newcastle, 23 September 1759, B.M. Add. MS. 32,896, ff. 52–53.
20. Namier, *Structure*, pp. 260ff. contains a detailed discussion of this affair; Pulteney to Bute, 23 July [1759], Bute MSS.
21. Namier, *Structure*, p. 170.
22. Paterson to Bute, 14 September 1759, Bute MSS.
23. Martin to Bute, 19 April 1760, Bute Corresp.
24. Martin to Bute, 30 August 1760, Bute Corresp.

## A NEW DIRECTION?

By eighteenth century standards Bute's faction was a considerable one.[25] It included a number of men of substance and several of real ability, particularly Elliot, Mackenzie, Mure and Martin. Unfortunately, there were others—Talbot, Carnarvon, Eglinton—whose warped enthusiasms were as great as their leader's and it was to them that Bute increasingly gravitated in 1759 and 1760. This was a reflection of the more extreme position favored by both Bute and the prince, and, in turn, it helped to feed the fires of that extremism.

The story of Lord Eglinton is illustrative of this tendency. Eglinton had succeeded to his Scottish earldom at the age of six, and had squandered most of his large patrimony before he was thirty.[26] He was proficient in dancing, riding and fencing, but his abilities were described by the Duke of Argyll as "almost useless."[27] In January, 1757, after years of dissipation, Eglinton announced to Bute his intention "to part with all my horses and turn Politician."[28] Bute, always glad to receive help, however dubious, welcomed Eglinton into his party.

Eglinton did not play an active role in Leicester House affairs until 1759, when he asked Bute to support his application for the vacant governorship of Dumbarton Castle, adding at the same time that it would be "greatly against" Bute's "interest in the west" of Scotland should another nominee get the post.[29] Bute wrote Newcastle on Eglinton's behalf and the duke replied that he would do all he could to obtain the governorship for him.[30] The earl also went through the formality

---

25. There were also politicians who claimed temporary alliance with Leicester House when it suited them. For the Townshends see McKelvey, "Bute and George III," pp. 268–69.
26. Sir William Fraser, *Memorials of the Montgomeries* (Edinburgh, 1859), I, 117–18, 338–39.
27. Argyll to Newcastle, 2 September 1759, B.M. Add. MS. 32,895, f. 135.
28. Eglinton to Bute, 2 January 1757, Bute MSS.
29. Eglinton to Bute, [c. 14 August 1759], Bute Corresp.
30. Bute to Newcastle, 15 August 1759, B.M. Add. MS. 32,894, f. 215; Newcastle to Bute, 15 August 1759, Bute MSS.

of asking Argyll's help, though he knew that his uncle did not favor Eglinton.[31]

Newcastle, for once, acted promptly. He first took the precaution of consulting Argyll, pointing out that the governorship would not only please Bute, but would also put an end to Eglinton's embarrassing bid for a troop of Scottish cavalry.[32] On the basis of Argyll's reply, Newcastle recommended Eglinton officially to the king, noting that the duke "did not disapprove it."[33]

Newcastle was horrified when, two days later, a relative of Argyll's requested the governorship from the king, "by the Duke of Argyle's order."[34] When the duke sought an explanation of General Campbell's candidacy, Argyll sent a most confusing reply.[35] Though Hardwicke and Newcastle were puzzled, particularly by Argyll's failure even to mention Campbell, they eventually decided that Argyll had acquiesced once more in the appointment of Eglinton.[36]

Acting on this assumption, Newcastle again sought the king's approval for Eglinton.[37] Despite the duke's frequent repitition of this request, the affair dragged on until, by the end of February, 1760, Newcastle was imploring George II to take action, "or my honor is sacrificed."[38] The king finally gave in, and Bute was notified that the appointment was assured.[39] But then Argyll returned to London from Scotland and told Newcastle that he intended to "wait upon the King,

31. Bute to Argyll, [mid-August] 1759, B.M. Add. MS. 36,796, f. 44.
32. Newcastle to Argyll, 29 August 1759, B.M. Add. MS. 32,895, ff. 7–8; McKelvey, "Bute and George III," pp. 271–72.
33. *Ibid.*
34. Newcastle to Hardwicke, 31 August 1759, B.M. Add. MS. 32,895, ff. 78–86.
35. Argyll to Newcastle, 2 September 1759, B.M. Add. MS. 32,895, ff. 134–36.
36. Hardwicke to Newcastle, 7 September 1759, B.M. Add. MS. 32,895, ff. 254–55.
37. Newcastle, "Memds. for the K.," 5 October 1759, 16 November 1759, 5 December 1759, B.M. Add. MSS. 32,896, f. 299, 32,898, f. 275, 32,899, ff. 308–9.
38. Newcastle, "Memds. for the K.," 25 February 1760, B.M. Add. MS. 32,902, ff. 388–89.
39. Newcastle, "An Exact Account of Every Thing that has passed . . .

## A NEW DIRECTION?

and acquaint His Majesty, that Lord Bute had set up the Prince of Wales's Standard in Scotland against the King; which was for the next Election. That they had already begun in Two Boroughs; And that, if this Government of Dumbarton Castle was given to Lord Eglinton, It would be a Declaration, in favor of that Standard." Newcastle pleaded that the matter had been settled before the question of opposition ever appeared, and that "My Word, My Honor, & Promise were concern'd in it."[40]

"I own I never saw myself under such Difficulties," Newcastle lamented to Hardwicke, "if the King should refuse me the Duke of Argyll would triumph, and Lord Bute not believe me. If His Majesty should comply with my Request, the Duke of Argyll would fly out; probably quit; And I should be reproach'd, by the King, for the loss of Scotland."[41] Hardwicke replied that all of Newcastle's problems arose from procrastination: "For God's Sake, don't suffer any more Delay," but present the matter to the king at once.[42] Newcastle, however, was too upset to rely on one man's advice. He sought out Lord Mansfield, who confirmed that Bute's "Flag is set up in other Elections in Scotland" and that Argyll was adamant on Eglinton's exclusion.[43]

Argyll and Bute were both determined. The duke, in a "very violent" humor, told Newcastle that any alternative was preferable to giving Eglinton the governorship. Dumbarton Castle was in the heart of the very area Bute and Eglinton were scheming to win away from Argyll; to give in to their demand would mean disaster. If Newcastle would not concede, Argyll

---

upon the Affair of the Government of Dunbarton Castle," 9 March 1760, B.M. Add. MS. 32,998, ff. 404–11.
40. Newcastle to Hardwicke, 28 February 1760, B.M. Add. MS. 32,902, ff. 453–56.
41. *Ibid.*
42. Hardwicke to Newcastle, 29 February 1760, B.M. Add. MS. 32,902, ff. 478–79.
43. Mansfield to Newcastle, 29 February 1760, B.M. Add. MS. 32,902, f. 484.

would have no alternative but to tell George II the whole story of Bute and the prince's electioneering. Newcastle protested that he was, with Argyll's expressed approval, absolutely committed. Argyll did not consider this sufficient.[44]

Bute's patience was also gone. He told both Viry and Lord Lincoln that nothing "but the Place" would satisfy Leicester House.[45] Bute was rapidly becoming, as Newcastle put it, "outrageous," but what was the poor first lord to do? Bute had made it clear that this was not simply a request from a humble Scottish nobleman, but "a Point of His R.H.'s; and how hard & indecent it was that a Point of the Prince's, not only promis'd, but declar'd to be done, should be stop't by the obstruction of one Man."[46]

Argyll agreed to settle for delay, promising that he would not approach George II until something could be discovered to appease Bute for the loss of Dumbarton. Time Newcastle gladly gave him. Completely disregarding Hardwicke's advice on the need for immediate action, the duke wrote on March 16 that everything "looks very well" and that a little more time should bring the matter to "a good conclusion."[47]

Newcastle may have believed that patience would solve all problems; Bute did not agree. On April 19, angered by the delay, Bute sent Samuel Martin to tell Newcastle that "Lord Eglinton had resolved not to accept of Dunbarton Castle," on the extraordinary grounds "that this appointment was not intended to be accompanied by the further support of administration . . . in the county of Air & district of Boroughs in it, against the D. of Argyle."[48]

Here the affair closed. Hardwicke still urged Newcastle to secure the governorship for Eglinton, so that the onus of refusing

44. Newcastle, "An Exact Account," B.M. Add. MS. 32,998, ff. 407–9.
45. Newcastle to Hardwicke, 8 March 1760, B.M. Add. MS. 32,903, f. 151.
46. Hardwicke to Newcastle, 14 March 1760, B.M. Add. MS. 32,903, ff. 272–73.
47. Newcastle to Hardwicke, 16 March 1760, B.M. Add. MS. 32,903, ff. 313–14.
48. Martin to Bute, 19 April 1760, Bute Corresp.

it should fall on Bute, but the duke did not dare face the king with the news that his grandson was supporting parliamentary candidates in Scotland.[49] It was not until June 27, more than two months later, that Newcastle finally mentioned the matter to George II.[50]

The cause of all this difficulty was simple. Bute was trying to undermine Argyll's influence in a number of Scottish constituencies, and the duke viewed Eglinton's application as a move in this campaign. Argyll's obstruction of that application, in turn, solidified Bute's hostility toward his uncle.

The two elections where the line between Bute and Argyll was most clearly drawn were for Ayrshire and the group of boroughs composed of Ayr, Irvine, Campbeltown, Inverary, and Rothesay. Together, these "burghs" sent one member to Parliament, the election being decided on the basis of one vote for each town.[51] The local magistrates made the decision for the individual boroughs. In 1754 Bute and Argyll had agreed on James Stuart Mackenzie as the member for the Ayr Burghs. The county, however, had been the scene of a bitter struggle between Eglinton and Lord Loudoun, with Argyll supporting the latter. Originally three candidates had stood for Ayrshire in 1754: Captain James Mure Campbell, Loudoun's cousin; Major Archibald Montgomerie, Eglinton's brother; and Patrick Craufurd of Auchinames, who had sat for Ayrshire since 1741. In April 1754, realizing that his cause was hopeless, Craufurd had given up his candidacy and formed an alliance with Eglinton. It was too late. Mure Campbell won easily, but Eglinton and Craufurd were determined to unseat the victor in 1761.[52]

49. Hardwicke to Newcastle, 20 April 1760, B.M. Add. MS. 32,904, f. 455.
50. Newcastle to Hardwicke, 27 June 1760, B.M. Add. MS. 35,419, ff. 233–34.
51. The Royal Burghs of Scotland were divided into districts by an Act of the Scottish Parliament at the time of the Union, each group sending one member to the British House of Commons.
52. This discussion of the 1754 Ayrshire election is based on James Fergus-

By the spring of 1759 Bute had decided to make an all out effort to gain control over both the county and Ayr district of burghs. This move was part of a general assault on the Argyll and Loudoun interests, planned by Eglinton and Bute. Since James Stuart Mackenzie had already laid plans for obtaining a seat for Ross-shire in 1761, Bute's first move was to ask Patrick Craufurd to stand for the Ayr Burghs. William Mure conveyed the invitation and Craufurd accepted on May 30, 1759.[53]

Bute was sure of one of the five boroughs, Rothesay. Argyll controlled two. Irvine was loyal to Eglinton. Hence, Mure wrote Bute, " 'tis only upon Ayr we propose to make our Attack, which is a *free* Town, under no influence but that of *internal Faction.*"[54]

Mure and Craufurd did not begin their "Operations" until August, when they received a letter from Eglinton assuring them of his interest in Irvine.[55] They then went to Ayr and secured a promise of support from the magistrates.[56] It looked as if the election were already over, but Sir Harry Erskine warned Mure against overconfidence. Argyll, he wrote, "is not a little chargrin'd at Lord Bute for this transaction." Erskine predicted, correctly, that the duke would attempt to overthrow the Ayr magistrates at the next local election.[57]

Only five days later Pat Craufurd confirmed Erskine's prognosis. The "Arts and Intrigues" of Argyll's agents, he wrote, had produced a new, uncommitted, provost in Ayr. Even worse, Argyll had convinced Sir Adam Fergusson, who had

---

son, " 'Making Interest' in Scottish County Elections," *Scottish Historical Review*, XXVI (1947), 124–27.
53. Craufurd to Bute, 30 May 1759, Bute MSS.
54. Mure to Bute, 4 June 1759, Bute MSS.
55. Mure to Bute, [10 August 1759], Bute MSS.
56. Craufurd to Bute, 22 August 1759, Bute MSS.
57. Erskine to Mure, 5 September 1759, in Mure, *Caldwell Papers*, Pt. II, 121–22.

numerous connections at Ayr, to run for Parliament on the Argyll interest.[58]

The battle was now joined. Craufurd, despite the personal intervention of Lord Loudoun, received new resolutions promising support from both Ayr and Irvine, "So that now these two Towns are as much fixt, as the Nature of a Borough will admit of, . . . for there is no Animal more slipery than it is."[59] When Bute wrote his brother how well the election was going, however, Mackenzie urged caution, lest Ayr or Irvine "be stole from You by the Old Practitioner in dirty Borrough Work."[60]

Argyll was undoubtedly a professional, but Bute's friends tried to make up for their lack of experience with enthusiasm. Even Eglinton reported long days of electioneering,[61] and the normally retiring Craufurd spent endless hours "drinking, hunting, and whoring" with the voters.[62] This attention may have flattered the townsmen, but they were more interested in patronage. Bute could offer the probability of a great deal in the future, but some immediate returns were necessary. Eglinton and Mure continually asked Bute's help in obtaining promotions or appointments for key individuals.[63] Some, two commissions in the marines, for example, Bute was able to secure.[64] He could never hope, however, to compete with Argyll, who obtained such favors from Newcastle in wholesale lots.[65]

By the fall of 1760 Craufurd's prospects looked dim. Argyll's influence had not yet secured Ayr for his candidate, but the

58. Craufurd to Bute, 10 September 1759, Bute MSS.
59. Mure to Bute, 28 September 1759, Bute MSS; Craufurd to Bute, 1 October 1759, Bute MSS.
60. Mackenzie to Bute, 24 October 1759, Bute MSS.
61. Eglinton to Bute, 23 June 1760, Bute Corresp.
62. Eglinton to Bute, 26 January 1760, Bute Corresp.
63. Eglinton to Bute, 2 February [1760], 23 June 1760, 9 August 1760, Bute Corresp.; Bute to Mure, 20 November 1759, in Mure, *Caldwell Papers*, Pt. II, 123-24.
64. Lord Anson to Bute, 8 July 1760, Bute Corresp.
65. Newcastle to Argyll, 23 July 1760, B.M. Add. MS. 32,909, f. 18.

vast amount of attention the burgh had received had turned the heads of the local leaders. By the time George II died, Ayr was still not assured for either Bute or Argyll.[66]

Closely related to the contest in Ayr was the election for Ayrshire, where Lord Eglinton's brother, Archibald Montgomery, was trying to unseat Lord Loudoun's cousin, Colonel James Mure Campbell. Loudoun had Argyll's fervent support, but it proved less effective than in the burgh of Ayr. Besides, as Pat Craufurd noted, Eglinton had considerable success in playing on "future hopes to raise the price more than his opponents can give."[67] The Ayrshire freeholders could recognize a sound reversion as easily as a London courtier could.

The prospect was for a very close election,[68] and Eglinton tried every conceivable means of influencing the voters. He even made an abortive attempt to renounce his own peerage, so that he could cast a ballot.[69] The extra vote proved unnecessary anyway, for his brother's prospects soon improved and Montgomery was returned for Ayrshire in 1761.[70]

The neighboring county of Renfrew was also the scene of a sharp conflict between Argyll and Bute. William Mure was the member for Renfrewshire, and he would probably have been returned without opposition in 1761 had he not sided with Bute in the Ayr Burghs. When a candidate appeared claiming Argyll's support, Mure went to Inverary to seek out the Duke. Argyll denied that he had yet given his backing to Cunningham of Craigends, but added that he "was excessively hurt" and "could not answer for what he might be obliged to do in order to defend himself from that unexpected Attack that was made upon him" by Bute.[71]

66. For the situation in Ayr in 1761, see W. L. Burn, "The General Election of 1761 at Ayr," *English Historical Review*, LII (1937), 103–9.
67. Craufurd to Bute, 13 May 1760, Bute Corresp.
68. Eglinton to Bute, 23 June 1760, Bute Corresp.
69. Alexander Montgomery [Eglinton] to Bute, 9 August 1760, Bute Corresp.; see McKelvey, "Bute and George III," pp. 287–88.
70. Craufurd to Bute, 21 October 1760, Bute Corresp.
71. Mure to Bute, 16 October 1759, Bute MSS.

# A NEW DIRECTION?

Despite Argyll's intervention, Mure was confident of success.[72] Bute helped by securing some crucial patronage for an important county family, and when the Head Court sat in October Mure's supporters carried every point.[73] Argyll, seeing that Cunningham's cause was lost, declared himself for Mure and the contest ended.[74]

Bute had an easier time in some other Scottish elections. No one dared challenge his nominee for Buteshire. James Stewart, a relation of the earl, was returned without opposition. Gilbert Elliot was assured of reelection for Selkirkshire. Sir Harry Erskine had firm control over the Anstruther Easter Burghs.[75] Sir James Campbell, "a Friend of Ld. Bute's,"[76] was unopposed in Stirlingshire. John Ross Mackye, who had represented Kircudbright Stewartry since 1747, received Bute's public support,[77] but it was superfluous,[78] for Mackye was returned without opposition. Bute's brother had an equally easy time in Ross-shire, despite an unexpected challenge from Sir Harry Monroe.[79]

Sir John Gordon had promised Bute his interest in Ross-shire, some six or seven votes,[80] and he counted on Bute's support in the Northern Group of Burghs in return. Despite the fact that Sir John considered himself a "tried and faithful Servant to Leicester House,"[81] Bute's aid was limited to assur-

---

72. *Ibid.*
73. Mure to Bute, 19 June 1760, Earl of Dundonald to Bute, 21 October 1760, Bute Corresp.
74. *Ibid.*; Mure, because of his appointment as a Baron of the Exchequer (Scotland), could not sit in the House of Commons, Patrick Craufurd was returned for Renfrewshire in 1761.
75. "Note of the Elections in Scotland," 26 April 1760, B.M. Add. MS. 33,049, f. 309.
76. Newcastle, "Memds. with the Duke of Argyll," 27 June 1760, B.M. Add. MS. 32,999, f. 17.
77. Mackye to Bute, 7 June 1760, Bute Corresp.
78. Newcastle, "Memds. with the Duke of Argyll," 27 June 1760, B.M. Add. MS. 32,999, f. 15.
79. Erskine to Bute, 31 July 1760, Bute Corresp.
80. Sir Robert Menzies to Bute, 28 August 1760, Bute Corresp.
81. Gordon to Bute, 9 November 1757, Bute MSS.

ances of goodwill, for Sir Harry Erskine had informed the earl that Gordon had little chance of success.[82]

Bute had a peripheral interest in three other Scottish constituencies: Clackmannanshire, Aberdeenshire, and the Stirling Burghs. Lord Cathcart controlled Clackmannanshire, and he assured Bute that his candidate, James Abercromby, was completely loyal to Leicester House.[83] Cathcart also had some influence in Aberdeenshire, which he offered to Bute to use at his will.[84] Bute apparently supported a friend of Lord Macduff's, Mr. Duff, but without taking any specific action on his behalf.[85] Adam Gordon, the Aberdeenshire incumbent, was reelected. Alexander Wedderburn was Bute's candidate for the Stirling Burghs.[86] Wedderburn was a young Scottish lawyer of great promise, and, when his prospects appeared slim at Stirling, Bute secured his return for the Ayr Burghs instead.

Bute was not involved solely in Scottish elections. William Mayne had his support for Canterbury,[87] but it did him little good, for he finished last in a field of four.[88] Samuel Martin had no difficulty in obtaining reelection for Camelford, nor Sir William Irby for Bodmin. Lord Pulteney successfully contested Westminster. All of these men could be counted on as Leicester House supporters in the House of Commons, but they stood for election on their own interest and in constituencies where Bute had little influence.[89]

---

82. Memo by Erskine, [late 1757-early 1758?], Bute MSS.
83. Cathcart to Bute, 18 October 1759, Bute MSS; Abercromby was elected for Clackmannanshire in 1761.
84. Cathcart to Bute, 28 March 1760, 4 May 1760, Bute Corresp.
85. Macduff to Bute, Thursday [April 1760?], Bute MSS; Macduff to Bute, 16 May 1760, 3 June 1760, Bute Corresp.
86. Wedderburn to Bute, 7 August 1760, Bute Corresp.
87. Erskine to Lord George Sackville, December 11 (1760), HMC, *Stopford Sackville* MSS, I, 45.
88. *Gentleman's Magazine*, XXXI (1761), 196.
89. Bute's father-in-law returned Lady Bute's brother, Edward Wortley Montagu, for the seat he controlled at Bossiney, but this was a device for foiling the young man's creditors; no one expected him to undertake a political career.

As his final exchange with Legge had shown, Bute had not given up in Hampshire. Hoping that the added time for organization would permit them to gain at least one of the county seats in 1761, Bute, Carnarvon and Simeon Stuart began planning for the general election immediately after Stuart's concession in 1759.⁹⁰ They even entertained dreams of securing part of the government's patronage, if Bute could exert enough pressure on Lord Anson.⁹¹

Carnarvon also had influence in Wales, as did two other Leicester House men, Lord Talbot and Sir Edmond Thomas. Carnarvon stood for Radnorshire, with the help of Bute and Thomas. Despite a suggestion that the Sheriff might allow his loyalty to Newcastle to overcome his honesty in counting the votes, Carnarvon won easily.⁹² Talbot's interest weighed heavily in Glamorganshire, and Thomas was assured of victory in that county when Bute persuaded Lady Charlotte Edwin to give him her considerable support.⁹³

Sir Lewis Namier has stated that "there is no indication whatsoever of any concerted election campaign by Leicester House in the summer of 1760. In Scotland alone, Lord Bute seems to have done some electioneering," and this "was nothing more than a local affair in which Bute engaged as a Scottish lord, not as Manager of Leicester House." ⁹⁴ In fact, Bute was involved in at least twenty elections by the summer of 1760, including thirteen in Scotland. In some he merely supported candidates standing on their own interest, but in many he was actively engaged. Bute's candidates were successful in fifteen of these elections.⁹⁵ Between the campaigning of 1759–

    90. [Carnarvon] to Bute, 9 December 1759, Bute MSS; 7 February 1760, Bute Corresp.
    91. *Ibid.*; Stuart and Legge were returned for Hampshire in 1761.
    92. Thomas to Bute, 18 October 1760, Bute Corresp.
    93. Thomas to Bute, 7 April 1758, 23 September 1759, 29 November 1759, Bute MSS.
    94. Namier, *England*, pp. 117–18.
    95. Craufurd was elected for Renfrewshire and Wedderburn for the Ayr Burghs, after Mure became ineligible for the House of Commons.

1760 and the election of 1761, however, a very important event intervened—the death of George II. The accession of George III undoubtedly influenced many elections,[96] but most of Bute's adherents were clearly on their way to victory before October 25, 1760. On the other hand, the accession also removed two almost certain winners, Irby and Mure, who were elevated to new dignities inconsistent with a seat in the Commons.[97] Had George II lived, the net result of the election would probably have been an increase of at least six or seven in the number of members of the House of Commons loyal to Leicester House. There can be no doubt that this increase was the major objective of Bute's electioneering.

Supporting parliamentary candidates was one way to strengthen the Leicester House faction; manipulating the heir's household was another. Prince Frederick, by making his household the heart of his political operations, had shown how important this latter could be. During his final opposition Frederick's establishment had included twenty-eight members of Parliament, the loyalty of each insured by patronage.[98] His son's establishment, on the other hand, was completely dominated by the Duke of Newcastle. All twelve of the M.P.'s in Prince George's household had been chosen by the duke, as had the two in Prince Edward's entourage.[99] Their loyalty was to their maker, not to the prince or Bute. If the prince wanted to declare his political independence, it was essential that he establish control over his own servants.

Prince George had enjoyed the right to appoint or dismiss his servants since his twenty-first birthday, but it was not until the fall of 1760 that he took action. On September 22, without any warning, "Lord Carnarvon surprised His Majesty

---

96. A number of other M.P.'s elected in 1761 were described as "friends" of Bute, but he had not been involved in their campaigns during the life of George II.
97. Irby became Lord Boston, Mure a Baron of the Scottish Exchequer.
98. Newman, "Political Patronage," p. 74.
99. *Court and City Register, 1760* (London, 1760), pp. 98–100.

by coming to kiss His Majesty's Hand for Lord of the Bed Chamber to the Prince of Wales," and Lord Pulteney was soon to follow.[100] The prince had taken the first step toward institutionalizing his political following.

The prince's initiative in appointing Carnarvon and Bute's electoral intervention are both indicative of a new, more assertive policy at Leicester House. Both stem from the prince's determination, encouraged by Bute, to escape from his "bondage" and from the "slights and indignitys" which he daily faced.[101] This new determination is also reflected in an increased hostility toward all who disagreed with the prince and his favorite, who no longer bothered to maintain even the pretence of good relations with their "enemies." Argyll tried twice to compromise his dispute with Bute, and was rudely rebuffed on both occasions.[102] The Duke of Newcastle was simply ignored by Leicester House. By September of 1760 he had "no dealings" at all with Bute and the Prince of Wales.[103]

Inevitably, this new "hard line" at Leicester House led to anger at Kensington Palace. When George II was finally informed of the full extent of Bute's electioneering, he was not only "most violent for supporting the D. of Argyll against My Lord Bute," but he also said that he would never agree to Bute's being chosen one of the Scottish Representative Peers in 1761, although the king and his ministers had already assented to his election.[104]

Relations between Leicester House and the government

100. Newcastle to Hardwicke, 23 September 1760, B.M. Add. MS. 32,912, ff. 47–48.
101. Prince of Wales to Bute, Seven [circa March, 1760], Sedgwick, *Letters from George III*, p. 41.
102. Mure to Bute, 16 October 1759, Bute MSS; Newcastle to Hardwicke, 21 July 1760, B.M. Add. MS. 32,908, f. 400; Newcastle, "Memds. for the K., 2 September 1760, B.M. Add. MS. 32,911, ff. 35–36; Newcastle to Hardwicke, 6 September 1760, B.M. Add. MS. 32,911, ff. 101–3.
103. Newcastle, "Memds. for the K.," 2 September 1760, B.M. Add. MS. 32,911, ff. 35–36.
104. Newcastle to Hardwicke, 6 September 1760, B.M. Add. MS. 32,911, ff. 101–3; Hardwicke to Newcastle, 7 September 1760, B.M. Add. MS. 32,911, f. 110.

were rapidly deteriorating. The approaching elections and a continuation of the prince's "house cleaning" would undoubtedly have widened the breach still further. This was precisely what Bute and the prince desired. In April, 1760, Prince George had written Bute that "my honour forces me to remain but little longer passive; my dearest friend I don't doubt sees the necessity of my taking a bolder and more resolute path."[105] By autumn the direction of this "bolder path" was becoming clear. It did not yet lead, as Argyll feared, to outright opposition,[106] but it did lead directly along the road followed by Prince Frederick in the 1730's. By asserting his own importance, the prince was necessarily challenging the role of his grandfather. Had George II lived, the 1760's would, in all probability, have seen yet another repetition of the traditional Hanoverian drama of king versus heir.

---

105. Prince of Wales to Bute, ½ hour past nine [23 April 1760], Sedgwick, *Letters from George III*, p. 43.

106. Newcastle to Hardwicke, 27 June 1760, B.M. Add. MS. 35,419, ff. 223-24.

# EPILOGUE

---

The years of waiting came to an end on October 25, 1760, when George II died of heart failure shortly after seven o'clock in the morning. His heir, who received the news while on an early ride, reacted calmly. Enjoining his servants to secrecy, the new king hurried back to Kew, where his first act was to write Bute, promising to do nothing, "till I hear from you."[1]

George III was finally king and Bute was his sole advisor. How well had their Leicester House years prepared them for their new roles?

Certainly the prince and his favorite had shown little political understanding. They had repeatedly antagonized George II and his ministers and gained little in return. They had driven away Pitt, Legge, and many others who would have been useful friends now that the "great day" had come. The twenty-two-year-old monarch was as little known to his subjects as he had been in 1755. And increasingly the prince and his friend had come to view their little court as the center of political reality, and to assess all politicians in terms of their relationship to that court.

All of this was far less important, however, than the ideas and prejudices George III and Bute developed during the Leicester House period. The half decade between 1755 and 1760 left the young king and his favorite with a legacy of hatred, bitterness and failure—but with their self-righteous confidence unshaken. This was a dangerous combination. Although George III continued his grandfather's ministers in

1. George III to Bute, [25 October 1760], Sedgwick, *Letters from George III*, pp. 47–48; Walpole, *George III*, I, 5.

office—given Pitt's popularity and the state of the war he had little choice—he immediately made it clear that Lord Bute possessed his complete confidence. The new king viewed his ministers as a depraved and treacherous lot and was determined to "make them all smart for their ingratitude."[2] This contempt for politicians, combined with his belief that Britain was on the edge of ruin, convinced George that it was his duty to free the crown and the nation from the "state of bondage" into which they had fallen.[3]

The result was personal and political frustration for a monarch who thought of himself as a moral reformer and national savior but who lacked any realistic plan for achieving his goals. The unhappy years at Leicester House were to prove a fitting prelude to a long and disastrous reign.

2. Prince of Wales to Bute, [22 December 1759], Sedgwick, *Letters from George III*, p. 35.
3. George III to Bute, [middle of November 1760], Sedgwick, *Letters from George III*, p. 50.

# INDEX

Abercromby, General, 87
Abercromby, James, 136
Aberdeenshire, 136
Aberdour, Lord, 126
Act of Union (1707), 3–4
Administration. *See* Ministries of George II
Admiralty, 54, 58, 110
Aix la Chapelle, Treaty of, 27
Amelia, Princess, 91
America, 27, 53
American Revolution, 103
Anson, Lord, 55, 137
Anstruther Easter Burghs, 135
Antiexpeditionary group, 75
Argyll, First Duke of, 3; and war with Spain, 5; personality, 4
Argyll, Second Duke of, 3–5; and Ayr Burgh elections, 131–34; domination of Scottish politics, 124; and Eglinton appointment, 127–31; and negotiations between Bute and Newcastle, 28, 39–40, 44; opposes war with Spain, 5; and Renfrewshire elections, 134–35; and Scottish elections, 131–35, 139–40
Argyll and Greenwich, Duke of, 3
Argyll faction, 125–26
Armagh, Archbishop of, 15, 58
Auchinames. *See* Craufurd, Patrick
Augusta, Princess of Wales, 14–16, 19–23, 32–48, 67, 79, 91–94, 109, 121; and Bute, 21, 35, 42, 48, 52, 57; and Cumberland, 16, 18, 55, 91; and Egmont, 26; and George II, 7, 12, 15–16, 23, 28–29, 33, 36–37, 45–46, 86, 106; and George, Prince of Wales, 34, 36–43, 94; and Newcastle, 14–16, 20, 26, 38, 41, 57, 92; and Pitt, 18–21, 43, 50, 92
Austria, 8

Ayr Burghs, 125, 131–34, 137 n. 95
Ayrshire, 131, 134

Barrington, Lord, 59, 74
Bath, Lord, 126
Battine, W., 110
Bedford, Duke of, 16, 24, 29
Berwickshire, 125
Billingsgate rhetoric, 31
Blackstone, William, 84–85
Bligh, General, 71–73
Bodmin, 123, 136
Bolingbroke, Lord, 8
Bolton, Duke of, 108–10
Boscawen, Admiral, 27
Bossiney, 125, 136 n. 89
Braddock, General, 27
Bramston, Edward, 109
Britain. *See* Great Britain, England
Brunswick marriage, proposed, 22–23, 93
Brunswick Wolfenbüttel, Duchess of, 22
Bute, Countess of, 3
Bute, Isle of, 5, 125
Bute, John Stuart, Third Earl of, 18–20, 24, 27, 29–30, 46, 54, 62–64; appointed Groom of the Stole, 12, 44–46, 49, 52, 89; appointed Lord of the Bedchamber, 13; and Argyll, 24, 28, 128–35; and Augusta, Princess of Wales, 21, 26, 35, 42, 47; character, 3; early career, 3–5; and Eglinton, 127–31; and Egmont, 26; and elections, 131–38; his "faction," 123–27; and George II, 31–32, 139; and George III, x, 141–42; and George, Prince of Wales, x, 34–45, 48, 82–90, 121–22; and Grenville, 31; and habeus corpus, 75; Hampshire election (1759), 108–11; and Holdernesse, 113–15; and Leicester House,

18, 20–21, 27–28, 34, 48, 90; and Mackenzie, 63; military patronage, 68–69; military policy, 69–72, 76; and Newcastle, 28, 46, 55–57, 59, 65–68, 91–97, 139; and Pitt, 19–20, 31, 49–53, 55–57, 60–61, 63–64, 67, 69–70, 73–81, 92–93, 97–101, 103, 113, 115–20; political opinions, 18, 22, 42–43, 63, 84–87, 121–22, 141; religious opinions, 88–89; and Sackville, 103–7; and St. Malo expedition, x, 71–73, 76, 78
Bute, Second Earl of, 3
Bute Manuscripts, xiii, 85
Buteshire, 125, 135
Butterfield, Herbert, ix
Byng, Admiral, 49, 53–54

Cabinet Council, 25
Camelford, 136
Campbell, Lady Anne. *See* Bute, Countess of
Campbell, Sir James, 135
Campbell, Captain James Mure, 131–35
Campbell, General, 128
Campbeltown, 131
Canterbury, 136
Canterbury, Archbishop of, 27
Carnarvon, Lord, 108, 122 n. 3, 123, 127, 137–39
Caroline, Queen, 6–7, 11, 28, 86
Carteret, Lord, 10
Cathcart, Lord, 125–26, 136
Cavalry, 76, 128
Chandos, Duke of, 108, 123
Chatham, 100
Cherbourg, 71, 73
Chesterfield, Lord, 9, 11, 54, 57, 125
Civil List funds, 7, 9, 33
Clackmannanshire, 126, 136
Clanricarde, Lord, 108
Clerk, Colonel, 71–74
Closterseven, Convention of, 64
Cockpit, 30
Coke, Lady Mary, 96–97
Common Council of London. *See* London, Common Council of
Country gentlemen, 9–10, 21

Court "party," 10
Craufurd, Patrick, 131–34, 135 n. 74, 137 n. 95
Cresset, James, 29, 48, 123
Crown Point, 87
Cumberland, Duke of, 33, 52, 68, 74, 77, 96, 120; and Augusta, Princess of Wales, 18, 55; commander in Germany, 54–55, 64; and Fox, 17, 50, 91; and Leicester House, 91; president of Regency Council, 18
Cunningham of Craigends, 134–35

Depot of the Sick and Wounded Seamen, 110
Devonshire, Duke of, 24, 29, 57, 102 n. 69; First Lord of the Treasury, 51
Digby, Lord, 65 n. 13
Dodington, Bubb, 15–16, 20, 29–30, 75, 77–79, 121; Treasurer of the Navy, 29
Dorset, Duke of, 53, 105
Downe, Lord, 68
Duff, Mr., 136
Dumbarton Castle, 127, 129–30
Dupplin, Lord, 55
Dutch army, 71

Edinburgh, 3, 18
Edward, Prince, 38, 94, 138; volunteers for navy, 67, 70–71, 73
Edwin, Lady Charlotte, 137
Eglinton, Lord, 127–34
Egmont, Lord, 20–22, 44, 48; and Princess of Wales, 26, 123; and Newcastle, 25–26, 30
Elbe River, 76
Elizabeth, Princess, 88, 104
Elliot, Gilbert, 18, 22, 42, 50–51, 110, 122 n. 3, 124, 127, 135; intermediary between Bute and Pitt, 117–18, 124
Elliot, Major General, 71
Emden, 70
England: constitution, 35; continental war, 49, 64, 68, 77; morale, 69; peerage, 22, 44, 65, 107; public opinion, 27, 64; subsidies, 24, 29–31; war with France, 23, 27. *See also* Great Britain

## INDEX

Erskine, Sir Harry, 58, 132, 135–36; and Bute, 54, 105–6, 122 n. 3, 124
Eton College, 4
Exchequer, Chancellor of the, 24–26, 44, 51, 55, 58–59, 78, 107
Excise, Commissioner of the, 67
Expeditionary forces, 70–74, 103

Ferdinand, Prince, 68, 74, 103–4
Fergusson, Sir Adam, 132
Fitzmaurice, Lord, 74
Fox, Henry, 16–17, 30, 36, 40–41, 49–51, 53, 55, 58–59, 78; and Leicester House, 16–19, 28, 50, 55, 91, 93; and Newcastle, 17, 20, 25, 45, 93; and Pitt, 17, 20, 50, 58; receives cabinet rank, 17–18, 30; resigns, 49
France, 69, 71, 114; fleet, 27; war with England, 18, 23, 27, 54, 69, 104
Frederick Lewis, Prince of Wales, xii, 6, 11, 14, 16, 18, 36, 65, 121, 123, 138; and Bute, 5, 13; and George II, 5, 7, 12; and the opposition, 9, 11–13, 33, 138; personality, 5
Frederick II (the Great), King of Prussia, 8, 22, 49, 62, 76
Frederick William I, King of Prussia, 8
Fryer, W. R., ix

Garter, Knight of the, 79, 104, 115
George I, 3–4, 6–7, 85
George II, x, 4–5, 7, 33, 51, 54, 62, 68, 76, 79, 86, 138–39; and Augusta, Princess of Wales, 14–16, 28, 31–33, 45–46; and Bute, 28, 31–32, 36, 44–47, 89; and Cumberland, 64; death of, 120, 141; and Fox, 55, 58; and Frederick, Prince of Wales, 5–7, 12; George, Prince of Wales, 7, 22–23, 28, 36–47 *passim*, 64–66, 94–102, 106, 140; and Hanover, 18, 22–24, 27, 73; and ministerial negotiations (1757), 58–60; and Newcastle, 38, 44, 50, 67, 94–97, 102, 128–31; and Pitt, 17, 28, 52, 58; and Sackville, 104–6; and Temple, 115–16. *See also* George Augustus; Prince of Wales; Ministries of George II

George III, ix–xii, 15, 120, 138, 141–42; and Holdernesse, 115; intentions on accession, ix, xii; political views, 84, 141–42; religion of, 87. *See also* George, Prince of Wales
George, Prince of Wales, 12, 19, 22, 51, 67, 71, 73–74, 77, 126, 142; and Augusta, Princess of Wales, 28, 37, 40, 121; and Bute, x–xii, 34–35, 41–43, 48, 59, 62, 69, 82–90, 99, 127, 141; character, ix–xii, 34, 83–84, 89, 141–42; disenchantment with politicians, 89–90; education, 34–35, 84–84; and George II, 7, 23, 28, 36–38, 40, 45–46, 64, 66, 94–102, 140; and Holdernesse, 114–15; his household, 14–15, 33, 35–48, 57, 65–66, 68–69, 95, 138–40; and Legge, 111–13; and Newcastle, 38, 56–57, 65, 91–97, 139; and Pitt, 52, 61, 77, 79–80, 90–91, 97–98, 113, 116, 119–20; political opinions, ix–xii, 43, 85–87, 121–22; proposed marriage, 22–23; religious ideas, 87–89; request for military role, xi, 6, 95–102; and Sackville, 102–7; and Scottish elections, 129–30; and war strategy, 69–70. *See also* George III
George IV, 6
George Augustus, Prince of Wales, 6–7, 12, 37
Germany, 8, 63–64, 75; British army in, 68–70, 76, 103; Pitt and, 63, 76, 79; subsidy to, 24. *See also* Ferdinand, Prince; Hanover; Hesse Cassel; Prussia
Gibraltar, 125
Glamorganshire, 123, 137
Glorious Revolution, 8
Gordon, Adam, 136
Gordon, Sir John, 122 n. 3, 135
Graeme, Colonel David, 69
Grafton, Duke of, 46, 65 n. 13
Grampound, 16
Granville, Lord, 51
Grenville, George, 4, 21, 30–31, 60; appointed Chancellor of the Exchequer, 58
Grenville, Richard, 4

Grenville "cousinhood," 20, 27, 51, 55, 78–79, 89–90, 115, 121
Groom of the Stole. *See* Bute, John Stuart, Third Earl of

Habeas Corpus Act, 75
Halifax, Lord, 24
Hampshire: dissenters of, 112; elections, 107–12, 126
Hampton Court, 5
Hanover, 22–24; antipathy toward, 23–24, 68, 86; defense of, 23–24, 27, 54; George II visits, 18, 22; neutralized, 64
Hanoverian heirs apparent, x, 7, 87
Hanoverian monarchs, xii, 57, 87; antipathy between generations, xi, 6–7, 140
Hanoverian succession, 3–4, 85
Harcourt, Lord, 15
Hardwicke, Lord, 81, 114, 126; and Bute, 59, 73, 94–95; negotiations of 1757, 58–59; and Newcastle, 27, 29, 32, 35, 39, 45, 50, 97, 106, 114, 128–30; and Pitt, 50, 60
Harrington, Lord, 96
Hayter, Bishop, 15
Head Court (of Renfrewshire), 135
Hervey, Lord, 5
Hesse Cassel, 24, 27
Hessian subsidy, 24–25, 27
Hillsborough, Lord, 20
Holdernesse, Lord, 51, 62, 77, 79, 96–97; and Bute, 114; and George, Prince of Wales, 114–17; secretary of state, 51, 113
Home, Lord, 125
House of Commons, 7, 17, 21, 29–30, 36, 40–41, 49–50, 76, 105, 107, 123, 125, 136, 138. *See also* Parliament
House of Lords, 13, 15, 30, 75, 85. *See also* Parliament
Howe, Lord, 71
Huntingdon, Lord, 99

Independent members of Parliament, 9
Inverary, 131, 134
Irby, Sir William, 122 n. 3, 123, 138

Irvine, 131–32
Islay, Earl of. *See* Argyll, Second Duke of

Jacobite rebellions, 85
Jacobites, 8
Jacobitism, 8, 10, 15, 124–25
Jenkinson, Charles, 73

Karen, vi
Kensington Palace, 36–37, 45, 139
Kew, 23, 37–38, 99, 141
Kircudbright Stewartry, 135

Lee, Sir George, 19–22, 26, 30, 43–44, 48, 123
Legge, H. B., 30–31, 50–51, 55, 59–60, 107–14, 126, 137, 141; and Bute, 24, 59, 78, 110–13, 137; dismissed, 31; Hampshire elections, xi, 108–13; Hessian subsidy, 24–25; and Leicester House, xi, 24–25, 90–91, 103, 113–14; and Newcastle, 55, 59, 78; and Pitt, 24, 60, 78
Legge, Heneage, 107
Leicester House, x–xii, 3, 11, 13–16, 26, 34, 36, 41, 43–47, 60, 62, 64–68, 75, 79, 87, 90–91, 102, 113, 121–23, 126–27, 136–39, 141–42; and Bute, 18, 20, 22, 27–28, 43, 48; antipathy to Hanover, 23–24; and Cumberland, 16–18, 50, 54–55, 64; and Holdernesse, 114–15; and Legge, xi, 90–91, 111–13; and Newcastle, 19, 26, 30, 37, 46, 54–57, 67, 93–95; and opposition (1755), 20–33 *passim*, 46–47, 49, 113; and Pitt, x, 20–21, 23, 26, 28, 43, 49–52, 60, 74–77, 90–92, 98–100, 115–20; and Sackville, 103, 105–7; and war strategy, 69–72, 74, 76
Lennox, Lady Sarah, 83
Leyden, University of, 4
Ligonier, Lord, 64, 68, 100, 120
Lincoln, Lord, 85, 93–94, 130
London, 5, 25, 41 n. 33, 60, 104–5, 107, 109, 128, 134; Common Council of, 105, 126; mob, 54; society, 125
Lord Privy Seal, 59, 115
Lords of the Bedchamber, 3, 65, 68–69, 139

## INDEX

Loudoun, Lord, 131–34
Louisburgh, 88
Lowland militia, 124
Lowlands (of Scotland), 125

Macduff, Lord, 136
Mackenzie, James Stuart, 63, 67, 122 n. 3, 125–27, 131–33
Mackye, John Ross, 122 n. 3, 124, 135
Mansfield, Lord, 39–41, 49–50, 58, 129
Marines, 133
Marlborough, Duke of, 40, 68, 70
Martin, Samuel, 60, 111, 122 n. 3, 126–27, 130, 136
Mayne, William, 136
Members of Parliament, 10, 98, 108, 122, 138; Scottish, 53, 124
Menzies, Sir Robert, 125
Militia, 9. *See also* Lowland militia
Minden, 104–5
Ministries of George II: under Newcastle, 22, 29–32, 36, 43, 45–46, 49; under Pitt, 51–55; under Pitt-Newcastle, xi, 60, 64, 66, 72, 74–75, 102, 105, 107, 110, 115–16, 121
Ministry of George III, 141–42
Minorca, 41, 49
Montagu, Edward Wortley, 136 n. 89
Montagu, Lady Mary Wortley, 4, 13
Montgomerie, Major Archibald, 131, 134
Monroe, Sir Harry, 135
Morton, Lord, 126
Mure, William, 72, 122 n. 3, 127, 132–35, 137 n. 95, 138
Murray, William. *See* Mansfield, Lord

Namier, Sir Lewis, vi, ix, 84, 87, 137
National party, 86
Navy, Treasureship of the, 29, 60
Netherlands, Kingdom of the, 115. *See also* Dutch army
Newcastle, Duchess of, 16
Newcastle, Duke of, 14–15, 17–18, 28–30, 52–53, 58–60, 62, 73, 78, 92, 114–15, 137; and Argyll, 128–30, 133; and Augusta, Princess of Wales, 15–16, 19–20, 29, 38, 41, 44–47, 92; and Bute, 39–40, 45–47, 55–57, 65–67, 75, 93–95, 127, 139; and Egmont, 26, 30, 44; and George II, 28, 31–32, 36–39, 41, 44–47, 97, 100, 102, 131; and George, Prince of Wales, 35–47 *passim*, 65–67, 94, 138–39; and Hampshire elections, 108–110; and Hardwicke, 27, 35, 38–39, 45–46, 96, 98–99, 114, 129; and Legge, 24–25, 55, 59, 107–10; and Leicester House, 19, 25–26, 29–31, 35–47 *passim*, 55–58, 67, 90–91, 93, 139; and Parliament, 21–22, 29–31, 40, 60; and Pitt, 17, 25–26, 44, 46, 49–51, 59–60, 77, 79–80, 101, 117; and Sackville, 105–6
Newcastle House, 20
Newman, A. N., xii
Northern Group of Burghs, 135

Opposition, 17, 52, 68; and Augusta, Princess of Wales, 14, 23, 28–29, 32; eighteenth century practices of, 8–13; and Frederick, Prince of Wales, 9, 11–13, 138; and Leicester House (1755–1756), xi, 21–33, 38, 40, 43, 45–47, 49, 51; projected (1759–1760), 121, 140; theory of, x–xi, 8–9, 43, 86–87
Orcades (Orkney Islands), 86
Orford, 108
Oswego, 49
Oudenarde, Battle of, 6

Page, John, 109
Parliament, 16–17, 21–22, 36, 47, 60, 115, 131; and Hanoverian heirs apparent, 6–11; Leicester House faction in, 122–25; opposition in, 8–10, 17, 24, 27–31, 40. *See also* House of Commons, House of Lords
Paterson, John, 105, 126
"patriot" policy, 8
Patronage, x, 10–11, 64, 80, 133, 135, 138; military, 68
Pay Office, 59
Paymastership, 17, 58
Peerage, 22, 44, 107
Pelham, Henry, 14, 16, 59, 73; and Duke of Newcastle, 15–17
Pembroke, Lord, 95–96

Peter the Great, 8
Pitt, Lady Hester, 49
Pitt, William, xi, 12, 18, 27, 30, 38, 70, 96, 104, 114; and Bute, 4, 19, 29, 31, 49–53, 55–56, 60–61, 63–64, 67, 69, 73–81, 92, 97–101, 113, 115–21, 141–42; formation of Pitt-Newcastle ministry (1757), 58–60; and Fox, 17, 20; and George II, 17, 28, 52; and George III, 141–42; and George, Prince of Wales, 60, 80, 82, 97–101, 119, 141; and Holdernesse, 113–15; and Legge, 24, 55, 59, 91; and Leicester House, x–xi, 19–22, 26, 28, 33, 43, 47, 49–53, 57, 63–64, 76–77, 89–92, 99, 115–21; ministry (1756–1757), 51–55; and Newcastle, 25–26, 44–46, 49–50, 57–60, 67, 77, 92–93, 101; paymaster general, 17
Pitt-Grenville connection, 78
Pitt-Newcastle ministry. *See* Ministries of George II
Pittites, 121
Place Acts, 33 n. 1, 107
Port of London, 107
Portsmouth, 70, 100, 110
Powis, Lord, 126
Powlett family, 108
Prado, Convention of the, 5
Prague, 60
Prerogative. *See* Royal Prerogative
Prussia, 23, 54, 62
Prussian alliance, 69
Pulteney, Lord, 10, 122 n. 3, 126, 136, 139

Queensbury, Duke of, 39

Radnorshire, 137
Rebellion of 1715, 3–4
Reform Act of 1832, 8
Regency Council, 18
Regency of 1717, 7
Renfrewshire, 125, 134, 137 n. 95
Reversionary interest, 11
Reversions, 22, 134
Rhine River, 76
Richmond Lodge, 13
Robinson, Sir Thomas, 17

Ross-shire, 125, 132, 135
Rothesay, 125, 131–32
Royal Burghs of Scotland, 131 n. 51
Royal Prerogative, xi, 8, 85
Royal progresses, 6
Russia, 24, 27

Sackville, Lord George, xi, 53, 57, 59–60, 64, 70, 89, 102, 116; court martial of, 104–5; and Leicester House, 64, 105–7; in war, 102–5
St. Clair family, 124
St. James's Palace, 50
St. Malo, x, 70–79
Sardinian Ambassador. *See* Viry, Count
Savile House, 105
Saxe Gotha family, 23
Saxony, 49
Scotch-Dutch Brigade, 69
Scotland, 3, 5, 13, 72, 96, 119; Act of Union, 3; cavalry of, 128; elections of, 124–39; Highland regiments of, 53; Sixteen peers of, 125
Scottish Representative Peers, 3–4, 125, 139
Sedgwick, Romney, vi, xii, 84
Selkirkshire, 135
Shelburne, Earl of. *See* Fitzmaurice, Lord
Shropshire, 126
Sixteen Peers (of Scotland), 125
Southampton, county of. *See* Hampshire
Spain, 5, 114
Stanley, Hans, 110
Stirling burghs, 136
Stewart, James, 135
Stirlingshire, 135
Stone, Andrew, 15, 19, 23, 26, 37–38, 41, 100
Strathmore, Lord, 125
Stuart, Simeon, 108–12, 137
Subsidy treaties, 30, 124. *See also* England, subsidies
Sussex, Lord, 65 n. 13

Talbot, Lord, 89, 123, 127, 137
Temple, Lord, 21, 30, 78–79, 116;

## INDEX

First Lord of the Admiralty, 51–52, 54; Lord Privy Seal, 59, 115
Thomas, Sir Edmond, 123, 137
Tories, 52, 85, 109
Townshend, George, 60. *See also* Townshends, the
Townshends, the, 24, 60, 127 n. 25
Treasury, 59, 118; Board, 24; Lord of the, 51, 56, 82, 92; "party," 10
Turin, Ministry to, 67

Union of 1707. *See* Act of Union

Viry, Count, 77–78, 91–93, 115, 130

Waldegrave, Lord, 16, 35–38, 45, 87
Wales, 137
Wales, Prince of, position of, 6–12. *See also* Frederick, Prince of Wales; George, Prince of Wales; George Augustus, Prince of Wales; George IV; Hanoverian heirs apparent
Walpole, Horace, 4, 21, 23, 35, 37–38, 123
Walpole, Robert, 5, 8–9, 11, 28, 86
War, Secretary-at-, 17, 59–60
Washington, Colonel, 27
Wedderburn, Alexander, 136, 137 n. 95
Westminster, 136
Whigs, 15, 51, 85, 108, 112; historians, 84; oligarchs, 22; rule, 86
William, Prince, 79
William III, 3, 24
Winchelsea, Lord, 58
Winchester, 108
Winchester, Marquis of, 108
Wortley, Mr., 4, 125, 136 n. 89

Yarmouth, Lady, 66, 100, 106, 118, 120
Yorke, Joseph, 114

Soc
DA
506
A2
M29